D1162597

Ernest Rutherford
and the Atom

Ernest, Lord Rutherford of Nelson
b 1871   d 1937

Pioneers of Science and Discovery

Ernest Rutherford
and the Atom

P. B. Moon

Other Books in this Series

ISBN 85078 187 6
Copyright © by P. B. Moon
First published in 1947 by
Wayland Publishers, 49 Lansdowne Road, Hove, Sussex BN3 1HF
2nd impression 1979

Text set in 12/14 pt Baskerville, printed by photolithography and
bound in Great Britain at The Pitman Press, Bath

Contents

Illustrations

Introduction

"If you take a little trouble, you will attain to a thorough knowledge of these things . . . So surely will facts throw light upon facts."

Lucretius, about 55 B.C.
(Trans. E. V. Rieu)

A pioneer, according to the Concise Oxford Dictionary, is the beginner of an enterprise, an original explorer.

Rutherford's scientific life was one of continual enterprise in exploring atoms. When he started, nobody understood radioactivity or knew what atoms looked like. By the age of forty, he had transformed radioactivity from a mystery into a steadily advancing science, had probed into the inner parts of atoms and had found that every kind of atom is centred round a nucleus, exceedingly small compared with the atom as a whole but containing nearly all its mass.

By the time he died, the field of exploration had moved inside the nucleus; it was known that the nuclei of different atoms are made up of different numbers of protons and neutrons, so that the problem then was not the composition but the detailed structure of nuclei. Thirty-six years after Rutherford's death, that problem is still not fully solved; research into nuclear structure has remained one of the active branches of physics and meanwhile the probing has gone deeper still, into the structure of protons and neutrons themselves.

It would be difficult to describe Columbus and his pioneering voyage to someone who knew little about ships and had no idea of the distance between Spain and the West Indies; a modern outline map would help, and something might be said about the navigation of those days and about seamanship. So,

The house at Spring Grove (now called Brightwater), Nelson, New Zealand, where Ernest Rutherford was born in 1871, looking rather dilapidated just before it was demolished in the 1930s.

Atomic power for generating electricity: This nuclear power station at Trawsfynnyd Lake in Merionethshire, North Wales was the first to be built inland. It was completed in time to start supplying electricity to the National Grid in 1965.

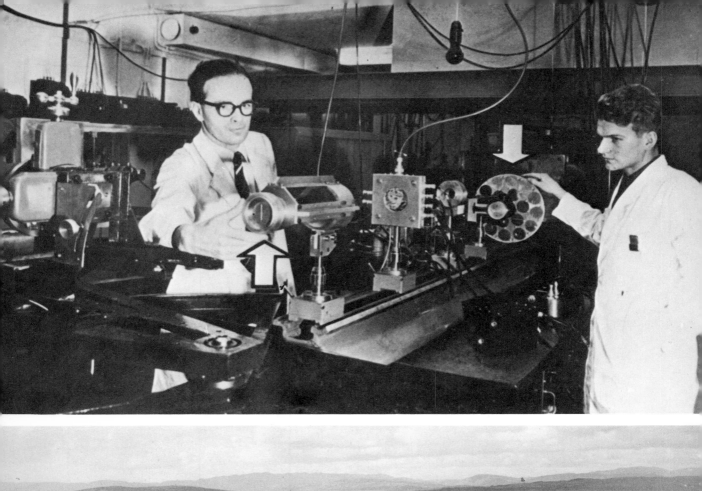

Developments of applied nuclear physics since Rutherford's pioneering work: The first known brain operation using a proton beam instead of surgical instruments was carried out on 22nd December, 1958, at the Gustav-Werner Institute for Nuclear Chemistry, at Uppsala, Sweden. The photograph shows the synchrocyclotron used for the operation and two members of the operating team.

H.M.S. Revenge, a nuclear powered Polaris Missile submarine.

assuming the reader to know a little elementary physics and chemistry, space will be taken now to give an outline picture of the world inside the atom, of which Rutherford was the first and greatest explorer.

First, the scale of things. A map of America in an average atlas will be about twenty million times smaller in each direction than the actual continent. If an average atom were scaled *up* twenty million times, its map could just about be drawn on a postage stamp or a penny. That map would show a number (varying between one and about a hundred according to the kind of atom) of particles of negative electricity—electrons—distributed about the atom. The correct symbol for an electron would not be a dot or a cross, but a smudge; though the word "particle" has just been used because electrons can be got out of atoms and made to travel like a stream of bullets, yet they have a somewhat indefinite size depending on how fast they are moving and, within an atom, the various electrons overlap one another.

What the map could not show is the central nucleus that was Rutherford's great discovery; on the 20,000,000 : 1 scale it could scarcely be seen by the best optical microscope. To bring the nucleus up to penny size, the atom would not be far off the size of Piccadilly Circus. Yet nearly all the "stuff" of the atom is in the nucleus, which is several thousand times as heavy as all the electrons put together. The nucleus is positively charged, and the atom is held together by the electrical attractions between this charge and the negative electrons.

Within the nucleus, our map would show a close-packed collection of particles—positively-charged ones called protons and uncharged ones called neutrons—held together, against the mutual repulsions of the protons, by forces that are not electrical.

Then, instead of Columbus's navigation and seamanship, something must be said about Rutherford's methods of deciding what experiment to do next and how to make and handle the apparatus. Nearly all his apparatus would look as simple to a modern physicist as Columbus's ship would to a modern naval man, but it had to be used with the greatest skill and perseverance. These are things that will appear as the story goes on.

Now when Columbus sighted land, he saw it with his eyes and knew what it was. Rutherford's view of the atom could be only in the mind's eye and he said that he used to think of an alpha-particle as a "small red ball." If the reader cares to think of protons as pink, neutrons as black, and electrons as green, no harm will be done provided, of course, that he does not believe they are actually coloured. Lucretius, who was explaining to the Romans the ideas of the Greeks who were the first to imagine everything to be made out of atoms, put it very well when he wrote, "Do not believe that anything owes the colour it displays to the fact that its atoms are tinted correspondingly. The primary particles of matter have no colour whatsoever."

Finally, a little about scientific words and about mathematics. As A. S. Eve wrote in his splendid biography of Rutherford, "If, every time he lectured, he had to explain the terms electron, atom, alpha particle, helium, gamma rays and so forth, he would never have got anywhere in his lectures. He had to assume a certain amount of knowledge, as well as intelligence, on the part of his audience. Yet people who would be horrified at ignorance of Shakespeare, Beethoven, Leonardo, Julius Caesar, will not turn a hair at showing the most profound ignorance about electrons."

The glossary on p. 93 is to help the reader who needs reminding of a word he has met but forgotten, or to give him the meaning briefly when a word has to be used before its meaning can be more fully explained. The definitions are not all completely watertight; some of them would be too complicated for the purpose of this book if they were completely accurate in terms of modern knowledge. I knew a schoolgirl who, being told that all atoms of a chemical element are identical, raised her hand and said "What about isotopes?" The reply was, "In the Fourth Form, they *are* identical."

As regards mathematics, there is almost none in this book, but Rutherford used mathematics well; without the mathematical knowledge he gained in early life he could not have disentangled the growth and decay of radioactive substances, or discovered the atomic nucleus.

Left
James and Martha, Ernest Rutherford's parents. This photograph was probably taken in about 1880.

Below
Like his father James, Ernest's uncle John was also a flax farmer at Spring Grove. Two of the workmen are sitting on iron flax-stripping wheels and another two are holding hanks of flax.

1 Career and Personality

Ernest Rutherford was born on 30th August, 1871, at Brightwater, near Nelson in the South Island of New Zealand, the fourth among the twelve children of James Rutherford, a farmer and miller of flax, and his wife Martha.

From the state primary school at Havelock, he went, at fifteen, with a Board of Education scholarship to Nelson College—roughly the equivalent of an English public school. The headmaster, W. J. Ford, had taught classics at Marlborough and was an exceptionally hard-hitting cricketer. Rutherford's parents

Wooden building of Nelson College where Ernest went for his Secondary Education, 1887–1889. It burned down in December 1904. There is a game of cricket in progress.

Nelson College.

Name _Rutherford._

Report for Quarter ending _June 27 1888._

SUBJECTS.	NO. OF FORM OR DIVISION	NUMBER OF BOYS.	PLACE IN CLASS.	REMARKS.
CLASSICS	VI	14	1	I have nothing to say, except that work is as good as ever; an occasional careless blunder is his only fault
ENGLISH SUBJECTS	VI	14	1	Works his to subjects up in capital style: has a retentive memory, a great power of reproduction.
MATHEMATICS	A₂	6	1	Very quick; a very promising mathematician. Has made very rapid progress. Easily first
MODERN LANGUAGES	French A	15	1	A very careful scholar whom it is a pleasure to guide in his studies.
SCIENCE				

GENERAL REMARKS—

His record speaks for itself

The next Quarter will begin on _July 27._ , when a punctual attendance is requested.

W I Ford

A midwinter school report on Ernest Rutherford. "His record speaks for itself," was headmaster W. J. Ford's comment.

Canterbury College (now the University of Canterbury) as Ernest Rutherford knew it in the 1890s. The Chemistry and Physics Departments in which Rutherford worked were housed in a huge "old tin shed" behind the buildings.

moved to the North Island at about that time, and Ernest was a boarder at the College. He was good at games, a member of the 1st XV, but quite outstanding in his studies, winning prizes or small scholarships in many subjects, including history, classics, mathematics and English literature. Physics and chemistry were taught, alongside mathematics, by W. S. Littlejohn; he found that Ernest Rutherford had great aptitude for these subjects and he spent much time with him outside the classroom.

After three years in this very good school, Ernest won a University of New Zealand scholarship which he held in one of the colleges that made up the University: Canterbury College, Christchurch. All students had to take a broad "pass degree" before

specializing, and Rutherford took six subjects, only one of them science. In his third undergraduate year, he concentrated upon physics and mathematics and graduated in 1893 as Master of Arts with first class Honours in both subjects. He remained in the College to work for the degree of B.Sc., which was awarded only after further study and research.

Rutherford used the high-frequency magnetic properties of iron to make a detector of radio waves; this was also his first subject of research at Cambridge, where he arrived in the autumn of 1895 to work under Professor J. J. Thomson as the holder of one of the scholarships that were (and still are) awarded to outstanding young scientists from the Dominions out of the profits of the "Great Exhibition" of 1851.

For a time, he held the distance record for radio signals, from the Cavendish Laboratory to the rooms of a colleague, more than half a mile away; and in 1902 he wrote, "I have however used for more than a year a device very similar to that employed by Marconi in his latest form of receiver—namely, an endless band of steel wire passing through the solenoid in which the electric oscillations are set up." This may well have been the earliest forerunner of the modern tape recorder.

It was early in 1895 that Röntgen discovered X-rays, and J. J. Thomson, though already interested in the work that led him to the discovery of electrons a couple of years later, took up with the help of some of his students a study of the electrical conductivity that X-rays produce in air. Rutherford soon became one of this group, and something will be said about that work in a later chapter, but the important thing for his professional career was the impression that his ability and energy made upon Thomson and others, for in 1898 he was appointed to a research professorship at McGill University, Montreal.

Rutherford's years in Montreal were full of activity and success; it was there that he and F. W. Soddy un-

Inside the Rutherford den at Canterbury College. The equipment shown is similar to that used by Rutherford.

ravelled the knotty problem of how various radioactive substances were related to one another. They were happy years, too; in 1900, he revisited New Zealand to marry Mary de Renzy Newton, to whom he had become engaged before he went to England. Their only child, Eileen Mary, was born in 1901; she became the wife of a distinguished physicist, R. H. Fowler, and the mother of another, P. H. Fowler.

Rutherford was offered professorships elsewhere, particularly in the U.S.A. where one university tried to add both Thomson and Rutherford to its staff at the same time, but it was not until he was invited to Manchester in 1907 that he left Montreal, already famous.

The invitation was made in unusual circumstances. The professor of physics at Manchester, Arthur Schuster, was a moneyed man. He wrote, in his personal capacity, saying that he intended to retire early; would Rutherford seriously consider succeeding him? Schuster could have had little doubt that the University would in fact offer the post to Rutherford. The offer was made and accepted; Schuster left in Rutherford's charge a fine department in which work on radioactivity was already being done.

The change from being a research professor, with no formal responsibility for a teaching department, must have brought its problems. Rutherford took his teaching and organizing responsibilities seriously but was able to continue research almost without a break. In little more than three years, on the basis of experiments done by H. Geiger and E. Marsden under his guidance, he had solved the central problem of the inner structure of matter; in his own words, he "knew what atoms looked like."

Rutherford remained in Manchester until 1919, when he succeeded Thomson as Cavendish Professor in Cambridge. There he died on 19th October, 1937. Life brought him the highest honours: a Nobel Prize, the Presidency of the Royal Society, a knighthood followed by the Order of Merit and a Barony, and finally, a funeral in Westminster Abbey.

I will not attempt to write in any depth about Rutherford's character; such judgements should be left to those with the closest personal knowledge. Nor have I anything to say about his attitude to religion or politics or to the fine arts, though he certainly loved literature and would quote from widely different authors; in poetry, from Spenser to Kipling. He was reputed to sing "Onward, Christian Soldiers" in his laboratory when things were going well, but this was not necessarily an expression of particular interest in Christianity or in music. Whoever first called him a "happy warrior" may or may not have been thinking of his war song, but the description fits him; he enjoyed his work and his successes and he kept going stoutly when difficulties lay in his path.

It is right, however, to attempt a sketch of Rutherford's appearance, manner and personality. As his close friend Sir Mark Oliphant has written, "he was tall and in later life bulky, but not exceptionally." He walked firmly and spoke and laughed loudly but not noisily. Oliphant says that Rutherford looked "more like a successful businessman or dominion farmer than a scholar." My own inclination would be to interchange the adjectives; when he was about in the Cavendish Laboratory in the late 1920's, his dress was tidy but not over-tidy, and his stand-up collar was already old-fashioned; his white moustache was stained by pipe smoking. Certainly he was far removed from the popular picture of a leading scientist.

Those who knew Rutherford feel an urge to pass on their impressions of a most remarkable man, telling stories of his energy, his enthusiasm, his frequent impatience and occasional irritability, of his concern for people and his gift of plain but vivid speech and writing.

His stamping-ground was what we now call

Ernest Rutherford as his research students knew him in the 1930s.

"nuclear physics." In this he was King of the Herd, knew it and delighted in it. He knew, too, that the young members needed encouragement, opportunities and (sometimes) prodding. Their life, like his own, must be full of hard work but should be enjoyed. He was a "good mixer" and he respected and praised good and enthusiastic work and play whenever he found it. If his enthusiasm, driving power and enjoyment as a scientist do not shine out in the following pages, I shall have done a poor job, but first I want to give a few examples of his dealings with people and his comments about them—and "people" will include Rutherford himself. They are in no particular order, but I hope they will show some of the reasons why he commanded so much respect and admiration as a person, giving much delight and, for brief moments, exasperation.

He was a great reader, and Sir Richard Southwell recounted how, at a dinner party, a bishop (or it may have been an archbishop) started to make conversation with him by mentioning a book he had been reading. It soon turned out that Rutherford had read it more thoroughly. The bishop, beginning to feel uncomfortable, said, "Of course, with my responsibilities, I don't have a great deal of time for reading." The devastating reply was "Yes, yours must be a dog's life."

Brought up on a farm, he was interested in things that grow, and, though Lady Rutherford was the keener gardener, he was fond of the trees and shrubs in their garden at Cambridge. After tea on Sunday when their guests were often a couple of senior physicists and their wives, along with three or four young students, he would take the men out for a stroll in the garden, sometimes talking science, but occasionally stopping to ask if they knew what such and such a bush was. He expected good and interested observation from his students, not only in physics.

As for work, my own introduction by him to

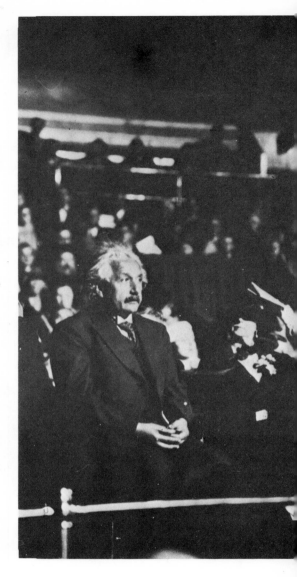

Albert Einstein (1879–1955) and Rutherford at a meeting at the Albert Hall in October, 1933, to discuss the problem of relief for German refugees.

Oliphant was typically pointed. "Moon, this is Oliphant; I want you to work with him. He's a very quick worker, and he'll tell you what to do. Moon ought to be all right, Oliphant; he's done Part II here." (Part II was the final year physics course, strongly based on a practical laboratory open throughout the week, in which the demonstrators included P. M. S. (now Lord) Blackett; hard work, mostly with very simple apparatus, was the order of the day).

Rutherford's care for people was shown in many ways, but often not directly to those concerned. He did a very great deal for the refugees from Hitler's Germany, finding places for some of them in his laboratory and scraping together what money he could to keep them and their families going until they could find established posts. He told me that one of them had come to him and said he had discovered something or other. "I stopped him short and said 'plenty of people know that', but you know, Moon, these chaps are living on the smell of an oil rag. They've *got* to push themselves forward."

As for himself, he was cheerfully but modestly proud of what he had done, and the typical story is that when the late Professor Eve (his successor at Montreal) congratulated him on some discovery and said "You're always on the crest of the wave," his reply was "Well, after all, I made the wave, didn't I?" Then he added, "At least to some extent."

Yet not even Rutherford could always be on the crest; troughs must follow crests in life as well as in wave-motion, and there was a time in the late 1920's when the work of his laboratory, and indeed progress in nuclear physics generally, was in a relative trough. His own great discoveries had brought the subject into being, and he felt in his bones that there were more surprises to be sought out within the nuclei.

With little but his own speculations to guide him and while improved particle counters and high-voltage particle accelerators were being built to attack the nucleus, but with no major results coming out, Rutherford sometimes confessed to doubts about the future. Langmuir, visiting Cambridge from the American General Electric laboratories, once found him in such a mood, and told him that when something new could be found, he would find it.

This prediction did not quite come true, but, as will be seen towards the end of this book, a burst of new discoveries came in the early 1930's headed by those of the neutron by Chadwick and of the positron by Anderson, Blackett and Occhialini; and the new era of nuclear structure research was heralded by Cockcroft and Walton's disintegration of lithium nuclei under proton bombardment. These discoveries meant, in due course, four Nobel prizes to members of his laboratory.

Something must be said about Rutherford's attitude towards other branches of physics. He saw to it that they were well taught to undergraduates, though he evidently did not believe in spreading his personal interests into other fields. He encouraged developments outside nuclear physics when men appeared who, in his judgement, were going to do big things. The best-known example was obtaining large resources for a gifted Russian physicist, P. Kapitza, who (like Cockcroft) had a flair for physics on an engineering scale. Kapitza wanted to generate extremely high magnetic fields and use them to study properties of matter, particularly at very low temperatures. The same example illustrates Rutherford's scientific generosity. On re-visiting Russia for a holiday, Kapitza was not allowed to return to England, and Rutherford agreed to let the greater part of the equipment go to Russia so that Kapitza's work could continue there.

In science, as in the arts, a few people stand out as greatest among the great. Within the limits of a single subject and of a period of time, it may be possible for

Dr. Peter Kapitza, (1894–   ),
Russian scientist whose work Rutherford supported, in Britain to receive
the Rutherford Prize for 1966.

someone who can speak with authority to pick out *the* greatest, as when Haydn told Mozart's father, "your son is the greatest composer I have known." (Remember that Haydn did not know J. S. Bach, and Beethoven was a youngster at the time). After the test of time, there are those such as Shakespeare whose position is almost unchallengeable; as Arnold wrote about him, "Others abide our question, thou art free." Newton is in that class too, and it seems unlikely that any modern scientist's reputation will overtop his. Where, in the perspective of a few decades, does Rutherford stand?

Lord Blackett has said, "In very different ways Rutherford, Bohr, and Einstein were the greatest physicists of the twentieth century." A risky statement,

Michael Faraday (1791–1867)
lecturing at the Royal Institution in
the presence of Prince Albert and the
Prince of Wales in February, 1865.

perhaps, because nearly a third of the century was still to come when it was written, but deserving the same respect as Haydn's about Mozart. Einstein himself said (and Blackett went on to quote this), "I consider Rutherford to be one of the greatest experimental scientists of all time, and in the same class as Faraday."

There is a notable comparison of Newton, Faraday, and Rutherford by Professor Feather, in which he says, "If my choice had been restricted to one name to set beside that of Rutherford, then surely I must have chosen Faraday's. 'The greatest experimental physicist since Faraday'—that is the common assessment of Rutherford."

Rutherford demonstrating deuterium reactions at a meeting of the Royal Institution in about 1934.

Though they were nearly a century apart in time, their talents and the magnitudes of their achievement were so similar that no excuse is needed for bringing Faraday into a biographical book about Rutherford. Indeed it is necessary to do so because Rutherford's career had its historical roots in Faraday's discovery of ions, as will appear later.

At this stage it is interesting to compare Rutherford with Faraday in their attitudes to honours and rewards. As honours came to Rutherford, he took them in his stride but did not forget the good start he had had at home and in his New Zealand education. When he became a baron, he remembered his home town and chose the title "Rutherford of Nelson"; and he cabled to his mother, "Now Lord Rutherford, more your honour than mine." Faraday, when sounded about a knighthood, said he would prefer to remain "plain Mr. Faraday," and he declined the responsibilities of President of the Royal Society though he happily accepted the many purely scientific honours that were offered to him.

Each of them gave service to national needs as well as to science; Rutherford to many official committees and during the 1914–18 war to the detection of submarines; Faraday most notably to improvements of lighthouses and buoys. These were virtually unpaid services and they took time from the scientific work that both men loved to do. Each of them lived modestly in relation to the place they held in national life; Faraday, indeed, gave up, at the age of forty, a large income from commercial scientific work in order to pursue his work on electromagnetism, but a few years later he was persuaded to accept a life pension from the government, and towards the end of his life a house at Hampton Court as a mark of Queen Victoria's favour. In spite of his reluctance to accept payment at anything like "market value," Faraday's financial circumstances probably compared well with those of Rutherford a century later, and his standing in national esteem was even higher than Rutherford's.

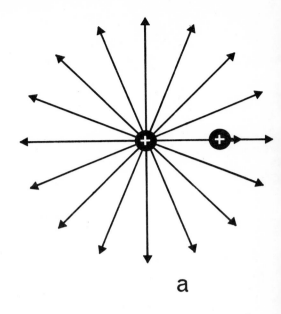

a

Fig. 1 (a) "Field of force" from one positive charge exerting a mechanical force (thick arrow) on another positive charge, (b) the second charge acting through its field of force on the first charge. If the charges are of opposite sign, the force that each exerts on the other is an *attraction* as shown in (c) and (d), with the lines of force pointing *towards* the negative charge which, because it is negative, feels a mechanical force in the direction opposite to that of the field.

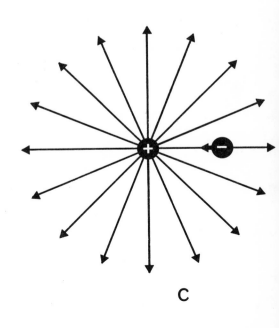

c

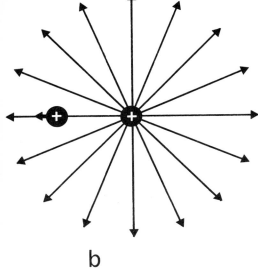

b

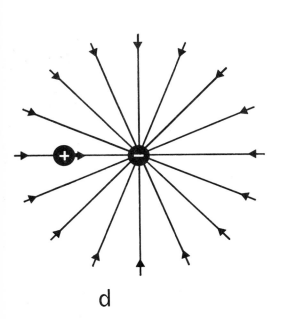

d

2 *The Scientific Background*

"If I have seen a little further, it is by standing on the shoulders of giants."

Newton.

The idea that all substances are made up of separate particles is a very old one, dating from the fifth century B.C. The teachings of the Greek philosopher Democritus on this subject (and on many others) have been passed on through a Latin poem written by Lucretius in about the middle of the first century A.D. Newton, writing towards the end of the seventeenth century, thought of these "atoms," as we should now call them, as "solid, massy, hard, impenetrable particles." Bosčović, a Croatian who was a Jesuit priest and who published a book on "Natural Philosophy" in Italy in 1763, appears to have been the first to believe that atoms must be quite different from tiny solid lumps. He thought of an atom as a point (in the geometrical sense, having no size) surrounded by what would now be called a field of force which could act upon other atoms causing them to "hang together" and form material substances. The idea of a field of force will be familiar to some readers through the examples of electric, magnetic, and gravitational fields.

In the electrical example, the experimental facts are that two "point" charges (i.e. charges small in geometrical size compared with their distance apart) exert a force upon one another, and that this force is inversely proportional to the square of that distance. We can think of a *field of force* surrounding each charge and say that the field acts upon the other charge (Fig.1). The fields due to many charges can be combined into one field; for example, if positive and

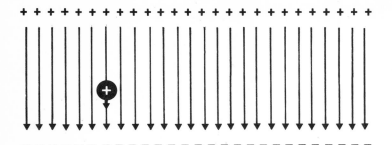

Fig. 2 A field of force due to two parallel layers of opposite charges, exerting a mechanical force on a charge between them. If that charge were negative, the force would be working in the opposite direction.

negative charges are spread evenly over two parallel plates that are relatively close together, the field is of the same strength at all places between them, and a point charge in the gap will be pushed towards one or other of the plates by a force that can be calculated very easily (Fig. 2).

Bosčovič's ideas are fascinating to scientists because they are so similar to the pictures of atomic structure that we use today, but he had no convincing evidence for them. Sound reasons for believing in atoms came first from the laws of chemical combination. The evidence, first expressed convincingly by John Dalton of Manchester in 1808, also showed that atoms are of many different kinds; a substance containing only one kind of atom was called an *element,* and during the course of the nineteenth century about ninety chemical elements, from hydrogen to uranium, were discovered, all substances being composed of atoms of these elements. The forces holding these atoms together were broadly described as "chemical" (e.g. two atoms of hydrogen and one of oxygen forming the molecule H_2O) or "physical" (e.g. molecules of H_2O or atoms of Hg (mercury) collecting together to form water or ice, liquid or solid mercury).

From measurements of the proportions in which elements combine to form chemical compounds, the *relative* masses of the various kinds of atoms were known to accuracies of better than 1%, but their *actual* masses could be estimated only by indirect methods

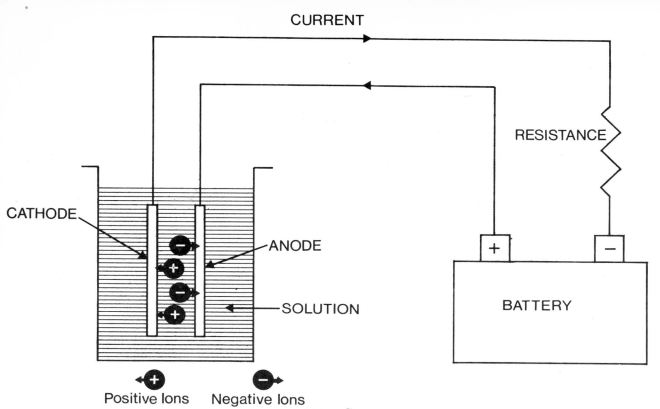

CURRENT

RESISTANCE

CATHODE

ANODE

SOLUTION

+ BATTERY −

Positive Ions   Negative Ions

Fig. 3 See text below.

depending on physical properties, and results differed by, typically, 20% for any one kind of atom. In the same way, a little but not much could be said about the sizes of atoms and molecules. This was a less important deficiency of nineteenth century physics, as it turned out, because an object can only be given a definite "size" if it has geometrical boundaries, for example a cube or sphere; it was Rutherford who was to show that an atom is more like a planetary system than a solid block or a liquid drop. Apart from this general knowledge of atoms, five pieces of nineteenth-century information can be picked out as particularly important for the future. Each is associated with a famous name.

1 Faraday and Ions

Many, but by no means all, chemical substances dissolved in water form electrically-conducting solutions. When a voltage is applied between two metal plates (the *electrodes*) immersed in such a solution (Fig. 3) there is movement both of electricity and of matter through the liquid. The movement of electric charge is seen as an electric current, and the movement of matter is seen at the metal electrodes in ways that vary from one example to another. For example, acidified water gives hydrogen at the negative electrode (*cathode*) and oxygen at the positive one (*anode*) while if silver electrodes are used with a solution of silver nitrate ($AgNO_3$), silver is dissolved from the anode and deposited on the cathode. With copper sulphate ($CuSO_4$) and copper electrodes, copper is similarly transferred. Faraday measured the currents and the times for which he allowed them to flow, and also the amounts of matter appearing (or disappearing) at the electrodes. His results could be expressed by the equation $M = Zit,$ where M is the mass of material, i the current, t the time, and Z the *electrochemical equivalent* of the substance in question. Now Faraday found his electrochemical equivalents to be proportional to the chemical equivalents (combining weights) of the substances concerned. For example, a particular value of the product of i and $t,$ in the neighbourhood of 100,000 *coulombs* and often called by Faraday's name, will be associated with the movement of 1 gram of hydrogen, 8 grams of oxygen, 108 grams of silver.

Faraday's own statement was as follows:

"Electro-chemical equivalents are always consistent; i.e. the same number which represents the equivalent of a substance A when it is separating from a substance B, will also represent A when separating from a third substance C. Thus, 8 is the electrochemical equivalent of oxygen, whether separating from hydrogen, tin or lead; and 103.5 is the electrochemical equivalent of lead, whether separating from oxygen, or chlorine, or iodine.

Electro-chemical equivalents coincide, and are the same with ordinary chemical equivalents."

Statue of Michael Faraday at the
Royal Institution.

Faraday saw that his results could be explained by supposing that the molecules of the dissolved substance (*electrolyte*) were separated into charged fragments (ions) that moved to the electrodes under the forces exerted upon them by the electric field between the positively-charged anode and the negatively-charged cathode. That explanation, plus some plausible chemistry, is enough to explain the qualitative observations. For example, if silver nitrate ($AgNO_3$) splits into ions of silver (Ag^+) and nitrate ions (NO_3^-), the NO_3^- ions reaching the anode can be supposed to remove silver from it by forming $AgNO_3$, which goes back into solution.

The quantitative part of Faraday's work was even more important. If we now take the example of copper sulphate and remember that because copper is divalent a "Faraday" will transfer not 63.5 grams (the atomic weight in grams) of copper, but only half that amount, we see that the Cu (and SO_4) ions must have twice the charge of their counterparts Ag^+ and NO_3^-. Everything fits into place on the supposition that electric charge is not infinitely divisible, but is as "atomic" as the chemical elements are. Given the ionic picture, nobody finds much difficulty in seeing how all this "hangs together," particularly with the help of the notation (Ag^+, Cu^{++} or Cu^{2+}, NO_3^-, SO_4^{--} or SO_4^{2-}) and with a diagram such as Fig. 4; but to have found such a simple and satisfying explanation of a behaviour not previously understood was a major achievement.

2 Mendeléev's Periodic Table

D. I. Mendeléev, though not the only scientist to notice the recurrence of similar properties as one goes from the lighter to the heavier chemical elements, presented these regularities by a table of rows and columns in which, with a few gaps and exceptions, the elements were placed in the order of their atomic

I	II	III	IV	V	VI	VII	VIII	O
1H								2He
3Li	4Be	5B	6C	7N	8O	9F		10Ne
11Na	12Mg	13Al	14Si	15P	16S	17Cl		18A
19K	20Ca	21Sc	22Ti	23V	24Cr	25Mn	26Fe 27Co 28Ni	
29Cu	30Zn	31Ga	32Ge	33As	34Se	35Br		36Kr
37Rb	38Sr	39Y	40Zr	41Nb	42Mo	43Tc	44Ru 45Rh 46Pd	
47Ag	48Cd	49In	50Sn	51Sb	52Te	53I		54Xe

Fig. 4 The Periodic Table of Elements.

weights. The modern form of such a table will be well known to some readers; for the others, a section of it will be enough, laid out in a way that will be useful later on when we come to see how Rutherford's discoveries opened the door to understanding it in terms of the structure of atoms. It will contain a little twentieth century information, but very little.

In Fig. 4, the letters in the boxes are the chemical symbols of the first fifty-four elements, and at the head of each column is a "group number" which is a rough guide to their chemical valencies, and to some of their other properties. The guide is a clear one at the extreme left and the extreme right of the table. Hydrogen, lithium, sodium, potassium, rubidium, and caesium are always monovalent; and all of them except hydrogen are metals. Helium, neon, argon, and krypton do not combine chemically, and while xenon is now known to be capable of some chemical combination the group is still quite fairly described as "the inert gases."

The important point, however, is that there was what Mendeléev called "a kind of periodicity" to be explained. It would not be explained without knowing what are the inner parts of atoms, what forces bind these parts together to form atoms and how two or more atoms can join into molecules.

Sir J. J. Thomson (1856–1940) operating an early forerunner of the modern cathode ray tube. Behind him is an electromagnet and in the upper background is an X-ray tube.

3 J. J. Thomson and Electrons

The third advance, which shed immediate light on Faraday's discovery of the atomicity of electric charge, was the proof by J. J. Thomson and others that negatively-charged particles—electrons—could be obtained from all gases in an electric discharge at low pressure. If a charged particle is moving in an electric or magnetic field, its path is curved to an extent that depends on its velocity (v), its charge (e) and its mass (m), as well as on the strength and direction of the field. By measuring the curvature in both kinds of field, the charge-to-mass ratio e/m can be found, though not the separate values of e and m. The value of v, incidentally, can be found too.

Thomson, working in the Cavendish Laboratory in Cambridge, measured such curvatures, and also the heating effects of the negatively-charged "cathode rays" from discharge tubes. His results showed that the e/m ratio was the same from whatever gas the electrons were obtained. Electrons, therefore, are something that all atoms have in common. Now the actual value of their e/m ratio was about 2,000 times that of the hydrogen H^+ ions that Faraday had found in his experiments on electrolysis. The simplest explanation, and the correct one, is that Nature's unit of electric charge is the charge, $e,$ of the electron, and that an electron is about 2,000 times lighter than an atom of hydrogen. The H^+ ion, then, is a hydrogen atom that has lost an electron; the Cu^{++} ion is a copper atom *minus* two electrons and the NO_3^- ion a collection of atoms (one nitrogen and three oxygen) carrying between them one additional electron.

Electrons, however, are not the only charged particles that can be obtained from discharge tubes. At rather higher pressures and with special arrangements for getting the particles out into a good vacuum, beams of ions, both positive and negative, can be obtained and studied. Their charge-to-mass ratios are identical with those for the corresponding ions in electrolysis.

Although the measurements with these discharge-tube ions were not made until several years after the discovery of electrons, they are mentioned here to show how well everything fitted together once electrons had been obtained free of their parent atoms.

The discovery of the electron as a free particle, the measurement of its e/m ratio and its recognition as a basic unit of atomic structure, were the culmination of experiments on gas discharges made by many physicists over several decades. We now have a look at two events of the closing years of the nineteenth cen-

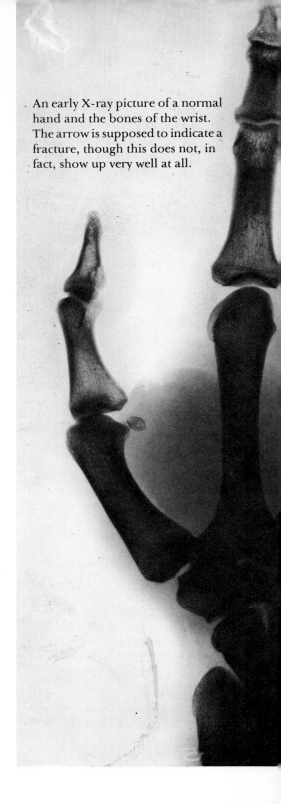

An early X-ray picture of a normal hand and the bones of the wrist. The arrow is supposed to indicate a fracture, though this does not, in fact, show up very well at all.

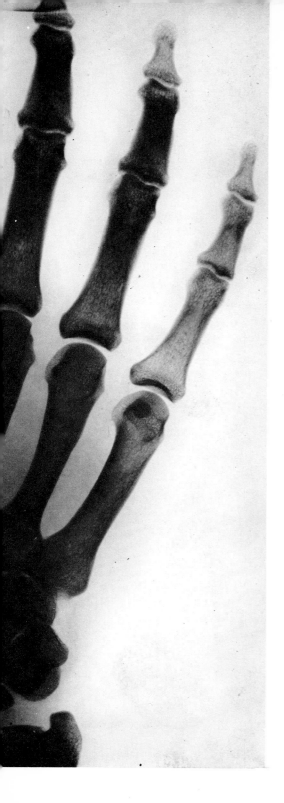

tury, which were discoveries in the most dramatic sense of the word—each unexpected and each the work of one man.

4 Röntgen's X-rays

In 1895, W. C. Röntgen at Würzburg in Germany found that photographic plates were "fogged" (i.e. the bromide emulsion became developable to metallic silver) by the operation of a high-voltage electric discharge, even though they were enclosed in solid material through which no light could reach them. In most languages other than German, where *Röntgenstrahlung* is used in honour of the discoverer, the unknown "radiation" was given the symbol X. While controversy continued for some years over the question whether they were waves or particles, and while they rapidly came into use by surgeons to aid in setting fractures, experiments with X-rays disclosed many interesting properties of which only one need be mentioned at the moment: they gave a small and temporary electrical conductivity to the air through which they passed. Thomson was apparently just ahead of Röntgen in noticing this, and when describing it to the Royal Society he said, "The passage of these rays through a substance seems thus to be accompanied by a splitting up of its molecules, which enables electricity to pass through it by a process resembling that by which a current passes through an electrolyte."

In giving this explanation, Thomson was going right back to Faraday; all that needs to be added here is that the molecules of the gas are split by the X-rays into positively-charged and negatively-charged parts, that these parts are naturally called *ions*, and that the positive and negative ions, just like Faraday's in liquids or those that Thomson and others studied in discharge-tube experiments, are atoms or groups of atoms that have lost or gained electrons.

5 *Becquerel and Radioactivity*

It was an experiment "about" X-rays, not "with" them, that produced the discovery on which Rutherford's life-work was directly based. In 1896, thinking that the X-rays might be associated with the luminosity that is seen on the wall of a glass discharge-tube running at low pressure and high voltage, H. Becquerel in Paris looked for a similar photographic effect of phosphorescence (i.e., the emission of light without heat). He actually chose what is usually called

During the First World War, X-rays were used in war surgeries. This photograph shows the interior of a German Röntgen field unit.

Henri Becquerel (1852–1908), who shared the Nobel Prize for Physics with Pierre and Marie Curie in 1903 for his discovery of radioactivity. Both his father and grandfather were also well known scientists.

"fluorescence," the emission of light by certain substances when they are illuminated by light of another colour, or by white light which of course contains many colours. Sometimes, the fluorescent light goes on for a long time after the original illumination.

Becquerel tried various substances, exposing them to sunlight and then putting them near to a photographic plate wrapped in black paper; he at last found a blackening of the developed plate when he used some crystals of a double sulphate of uranium and potassium which had been grown many years before by his father. Repeating the experiment on a dull day, he found just as much blackening, so the effect was not due to anything that sunlight had done to the crystals but to a property of the crystals themselves; they emitted some "radiation" that could pass through solids, just as X-rays do. Becquerel soon found that all compounds of uranium gave the same effect, so clearly it was a property of uranium and had nothing to do with phosphorescence.

"Radio-activity," later written as "radioactivity," was the name given to this remarkable behaviour of uranium. The similarity of the action of uranium radiation to X-rays was not limited to their photographic effect; for example, Becquerel found that air in the neighbourhood of a uranium compound had a weak but measurable electrical conductivity. We shall see that this conductivity led Marie Curie to the discovery of new radioactive elements, and that its careful study by Rutherford showed that, though the conductivities produced by X-rays and by radioactivity were very similar, the radiations producing the conductivity were quite different.

3 *Ionization, Rays, and Emanations*

"O my darlings, O my darlings, O my darling ions mine,
You are lost and gone for ever, when just once you recombine."

Cavendish Laboratory Songbook.

By the autumn of 1897, Rutherford had been two years in the Cavendish Laboratory, working on radio waves but surrounded by the excitement of Thomson's discovery of the electron. The electrical conductivity of air when exposed to X-rays, interpreted by Thomson as being due to the formation of ions in the air, was another main interest of the Laboratory.

Now Rutherford knew that the radioactivity of uranium gave a similar conductivity, and so did ultra-violet light. He started to compare the electrical conductivities produced by these three. If Thomson was right about ions, there should be strong similarities; if the same numbers of the same kinds of ion were produced, the conductivity should be just the same, whether caused by radioactivity, X-rays or light. The comparison soon narrowed itself down to X-rays and radioactivity, for ultra-violet light releases charges from solid and liquid surfaces more than from within gases, and in the end Rutherford's interest became fixed on radioactivity, while others went on with the study of ions produced by X-rays.

A view of Great Court, Trinity College, Cambridge, taken in the late nineteenth century.

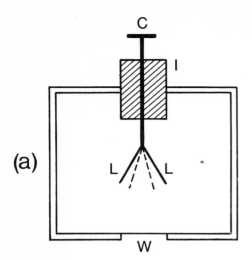

(a)

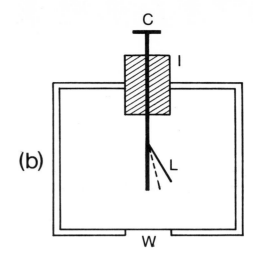

(b)

Fig. 5 Gold-leaf electroscope. L—leaf, C—charging cap, I—insulator, W—window. The double-leaf type is shown at (a) and the single-leaf at (b).

The instrument with which the conductivity was most simply measured was a gold-leaf electroscope (Fig. 5). When an electric charge is put on the leaves by way of the charging knob, they repel one another. If ions are present in the gas, the electric field between leaves and case makes the positive and negative ions move in opposite directions, and as ions reach the leaves the original charge is gradually neutralized, so the leaves gradually come together again.

The collapse of the leaves from one position (full lines) to another (broken lines) corresponds to the collection of a fixed amount of charge; that is to say, the amount of charge collected by the leaves must be the same for the same electroscope and the same two positions, whatever the cause of the conductivity. Here we have a very simple, if not very accurate, way of measuring small charges; simple because anybody who can obtain some gold-leaf and a good insulator can make one, not very accurate because the tip of the leaf seen through a low-power microscope with an eyepiece scale is not an ideal "pointer."

The trouble starts when we ask whether all the ions that are formed in the gas are collected; the answer is yes, provided the electric field sweeps them through the gas before positive and negative ones meet one

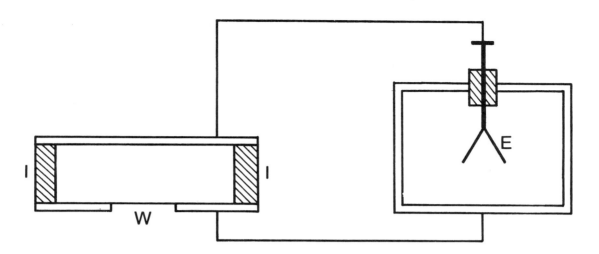

Fig. 6 Ionization chamber (W—window, I—insulator) connected to electroscope E.

another and recombine to form neutral molecules again; ions, just like ordinary molecules, are continually moving around at quite high speeds.

Now the field is strong near the leaves and weakens as you go away from them, particularly towards the corners of the box. It is not practical to increase the charge on the leaves until the field is strong enough everywhere in the box, for the leaves would then stand out almost horizontally and in that position a small change in their charge makes very little difference; the instrument becomes insensitive. The answer to the problem is to collect the ions in a separate "ionization chamber" (Fig. 6) made of two parallel metal plates, and to connect the electroscope across them, like a voltmeter. The body of the electroscope is made thick enough to prevent any ionization within it and the bottom of the ionization chamber can be given a thin "window," say of aluminium foil, so that whatever radiation is being studied, it has no difficulty in getting through. As the technique developed, more accurate electrometers were substituted for the simple electroscopes.

Unlike the situation in an electrolyte, where ions are always present in large numbers and there is no particular limit to the current that may be drawn, a quite moderate voltage will draw across all the ions that are produced by a layer of, say, a uranium compound placed below the window, or by a not-too-powerful X-ray tube at some distance away. It is this "saturation current" that is the measure of the rate at which ions are being produced in the chamber.

Now when Rutherford placed radioactive substances beneath the window and then put "absorbers" in between the two, he found that part of the ionizing radiation was stopped by very thin absorbers but part was more penetrating. In words written later:

"These experiments show that the uranium radiation is complex and that there are present at least two distinct types of radiation—one that is very easily absorbed, which for convenience will be termed the α-radiation, and the other of a more penetrative character, which will be termed the β-radiation."

A still more penetrating type of radiation, gamma-rays, was discovered a little later when Villard made experiments similar to Rutherford's but with thicker absorbers. The alpha-rays were so strongly absorbed that Rutherford soon put the uranium compound *inside* the ionization chamber.

Now, Rutherford did not invent the electroscope or the ionization chamber and he was not the first to find a difference between the radiations from uranium; Becquerel had found that some (the β-rays) could be deflected by a magnetic field, and others apparently not. Why, then, take space to describe how these ionization experiments were done?

First, Rutherford was learning new techniques, very different from those of the radio work that had drawn attention to him and won him the scholarship that brought him to England. Secondly, he was moving very rapidly; he did a great deal of work with X-ray ionization as well as with radioactivity in about a year, checking in considerable detail that the conductivity corresponded with what would be expected in the

Marie Curie (1867–1934) who, with her husband Pierre (1859–1906) discovered polonium and radium in 1898. For this they jointly won the

Nobel Prize for Physics in 1903. In 1911, Marie also won the chemistry prize, one of the very few people ever to receive two Nobel prizes.

"ion" picture. "A very fast worker" was what he liked to be able to say in later years about his own best students, and he was showing himself to be a very fast worker indeed. The success of this third year in Cambridge added so much to Rutherford's reputation that Thomson, with a little doubt at first but then with strong support, recommended him for a big step in his professional career. He wrote, "I have never had a student with more enthusiasm or ability than Mr Rutherford and I am sure that if elected he would establish a distinguished school of Physics at Montreal".

In the summer of 1898, having written a long (and famous) paper describing his ionization experiments, Rutherford left Cambridge for Montreal, where he had been appointed to a research professorship at McGill University. In the meantime thorium had been found by Schmidt and Marie Curie to show radioactivity comparable with that of uranium, and Rutherford ordered both uranium and thorium salts for his work. Though they did not reach him until well after his own arrival, he got to work again so rapidly that in May 1899 he had sent out for publication a paper entitled "Uranium and Thorium Radioactivity."

Mme. Curie had, however, done much more than finding radioactivity in thorium. In 1898, she and her husband Pierre had found that, weight for weight of uranium content, some uranium minerals were more active than uranium itself. Now for pure uranium compounds made in the laboratory, the activity had been found by Becquerel to be exactly proportional to the content of uranium, and therefore to be a property of the uranium atoms themselves. It seemed to follow that the minerals must contain strongly radioactive elements, present in very small amounts because the chemical analyses of the minerals showed only "ordinary" elements apart from uranium and thorium. The story of the extraction from pitchblende

45

first of polonium and then of radium need not be repeated here, but it is worth emphasizing that the process was followed throughout by ionization measurements.

In due course, Rutherford obtained a quantity of radium, which in solution (as chloride or bromide) was the basic source of radioactive materials for most of his work in Montreal, as indeed were such solutions for his later work in Manchester and in his second Cambridge period. Now before leaving Cambridge, Rutherford had noticed that thorium nitrate, and particularly thorium oxide, when exposed to the air on a platinum plate, gave an ionizing radiation that varied in an apparently haphazard manner with time. In Montreal, he studied this carefully and was able to write in September 1899 that "In addition to their ordinary radiation, I have found that thorium compounds continuously emit radioactive particles of some kind, which retain their radioactive powers for several minutes." The particles finally proved to be atoms of an inert gas, first called "thorium emanation" and later christened "thoron," into which thorium atoms are transformed as they emit the α-rays that are the "ordinary radiation" from thorium; but this was not understood until a few years later when Rutherford established that radioactivity is the spontaneous transformation of one type of atom into others. This is mentioned now to show Rutherford's great talent for dealing with complicated experimental situations and getting important results from them; in this case, the haphazard behaviour was due to the slow diffusion of the gas out of the solid and to its being carried about the laboratory by air currents; but there was also a basic complexity because, once produced, the thoron itself underwent radioactive change and deposited solid radioactive materials on surfaces with which it came into contact.

The Cavendish Laboratory, Free School Lane, Cambridge, where Rutherford was a student and later, Professor of Experimental Physics.

4 Atoms in Decay

"O change beyond report, thought, or belief!"
Milton

We have seen how, in his last year as a graduate student in Cambridge and his first three years or so as a professor in Montreal, Rutherford had mastered the techniques of the ionization method of measuring radioactivity and had distinguished the strongly ionizing, readily absorbed α-rays from the less ionizing, more penetrating β-rays. The rapid loss of kinetic energy, resulting from the ionization of the medium through which it passes, brings an α-ray to rest after passing through matter a distance about equal to the thickness of a sheet of paper. He had also discovered, but had not yet understood, the emanation that accompanied the primary radioactivity of thorium, and he had learned something about the radioactive deposit left by the emanation on surfaces with which it came into contact.

In 1901, in collaboration with Frederick Soddy, Rutherford launched a thorough attack on the emanation problem. They found that the emanation, once it had left the thorium compound, could pass unchanged through chemical reagents of all types and at various temperatures, whether it was initially carried by air or by other gases in which the thorium compound was immersed. In their paper published by the Chemical Society (London) in the spring of 1902 they commented that, "The only gases capable of passing in unchanged amount through all the reagents employed are the recently discovered gases of the argon family," and they concluded that, "the emanation is a chemically inert gas analogous in nature to the members of the argon family." This newly discovered gas soon became known as thoron.

(Argon was discovered by Rayleigh in 1896. For the other inert gases, see Fig. 4).

Now it is just because of its chemical inertness that thoron (and a corresponding gas, radon, accompanying the radioactivity of radium) could be separated fairly cleanly from its parent substance, though the actual amounts of emanation were unweighably small. The next, and more difficult, task was to learn more about the radioactivity deposited by the emanation on solid surfaces. If it is a substance, it must have some chemical properties, so Rutherford and Soddy tried to extract, by chemical means, radioactive substances from solid thorium salts out of which the thoron had not diffused. In this they were essentially following the path of the Curies in their extraction of polonium and radium from uranium ores. They met severe difficulties but were able to concentrate into small bulk much of the activity corresponding to the deposit (which they first called "excited radioactivity") as well as some corresponding to the emanation. They realized that the difficulties besetting them, which had not seriously beset the Curies, arose because of the extremely small amounts of matter they were putting through chemical processes. They wrote about the "emanating substance" making its appearance "dragged down by precipitates when no question of insolubility is involved."

In spite of difficulties, Rutherford and Soddy managed to get repeatable and very remarkable results from other chemical operations. They found, firstly, that the greater part of the ionization produced by a sample of "thorium" that had been undisturbed for a long time was not due to "thorium" but to some other substance that could be separated from it. The same applied to the ability of "thorium" to produce the radioactive emanation that escaped into the air; indeed practically the whole of the emanating power belonged to some chemically different substance.

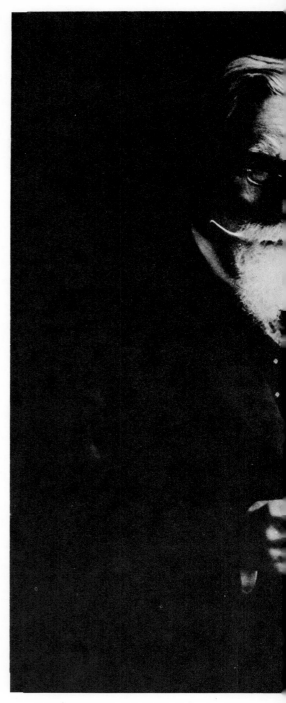

Sir William Crookes (1832–1919), British physicist and chemist.

48

This substance was *relatively* very much more radioactive than "thorium," for the amount of it was unweighably small.

The activity of the separated substance, as measured by the ionization it produced, did not remain constant but decayed with time; and as it decayed so did the "thorium," from which it had been separated, recover its activity and its power of producing emanation. (Thorium is put between inverted commas because radiothorium, which is chemically *in*separable from thorium, was in fact the main source of the activity that remained with the thorium when the separation was made). They gave the name "thorium X" to the substance that was producing the emanation.

They were not the only scientists to meet similar puzzling effects: Becquerel himself had prepared an inactive uranium nitrate which recovered its activity after a time, and Sir William Crookes in London had separated a highly active constituent from uranium. Rutherford and Soddy, with vigour and sheer hard work as well as Rutherford's characteristic ability to pick out essential points, went further and faster and arrived at the correct conclusion that one radioactive substance was generating another in a series of successive transformations. Many of the experiments concerning thorium were published in July 1902, but their full and clear interpretation did not come until nearly a year later, though in the meantime Rutherford and Soddy had been writing confidently that "these changes must be occurring within the atom, and the radioactive elements must be undergoing spontaneous transformation." In 1903, they were ready to emphasize that the radiations must accompany the corresponding atomic transformation, i.e., each α- or β-ray must be emitted by a single atom at the instant of transformation.

To the extent, and it was quite considerable, that they could follow the decay of a single activity apart

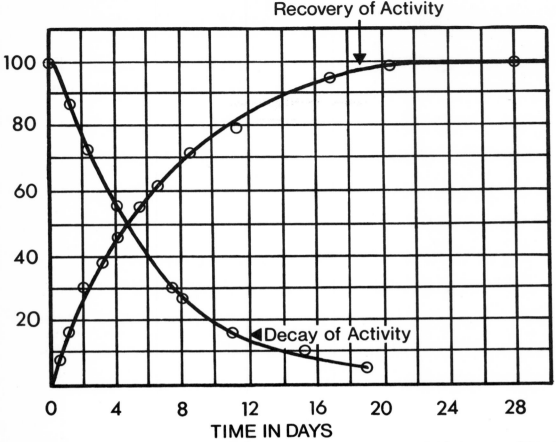

Recovery of Activity

◄Decay of Activity

TIME IN DAYS

Fig. 7 The decay curve of chemically separated thorium X and the recovery of activity in the substance from which the thorium X had been separated.

from effects due to preceding or following substances, they found that it followed what they described as a "geometric progression with time," by which was meant a drop in activity by a fixed factor in each equal interval of time. This we would now call an "exponential decay" and it was matched by an exponential recovery of activity in the "mother" substance (Fig. 7). The time taken to fall, or rise, to half the full activity was called the "half life;" it was about four days for the "emanating substance" (Th X) and about a minute for the emanation itself.

It was a great achievement to have discovered that the principle of an exponential decay, with a half-life different for each substance, would explain the complex patterns of growth and decay that they observed. They had at the time put their fingers on only a few of the main characters in the mystery: the "emanating substance" (Th X), the "emanation" (Tn), and two groups of radioactive substances following it, which were first called "excited radioactivities" but soon became known as the "active deposit." Fig. 8 shows the state of their knowledge in 1903.

They worked out, in full mathematical detail, the theory of the growth and decay of any one of a series of activities as it was produced by its "parent" and in turn produced its "daughter." This is too complicated to give here, but it is an enduring monument to Rutherford and Soddy.

The first three years of the twentieth century, when Rutherford was about thirty, were probably the most vigorously active of his scientific life. To show the amount of work he produced, often with Soddy but sometimes by himself, the publications in the peak year of 1903 can be taken. Publishing his results was important to Rutherford; he knew he was in the lead and he was always quick to put into print what he had achieved. Yet, with all the volume of writing and all the work and thought that lay behind it, the quality of his wording was outstanding. Some of the words and phrases may look old-fashioned now, but the style is impressively direct and forceful.

As this time, Rutherford was publishing mostly in the *Philosophical Magazine,* a monthly journal of physics; the title dates back to times when physics was called "Natural Philosophy." In the first six issues for 1903 there were no less than seven articles, some of them nearly half the length of this book, by Rutherford and those who were working with him in Montreal. They were well-written, full of experimental details and keen and logical discussion of the results. In later years, when he sent important papers from his Cambridge laboratory to be published in the *Proceedings of the Royal Society,* Rutherford said, "If one of my boys publishes *one* good Royal Society paper a year, he's doing well.''

The titles of these papers included "Excited Radioactivity," "Magnetic and Electric Deviation of the Easily Absorbed Rays From Radium," "Condensation of the Radioactive Emanations" and three papers concerned with the radioactivities of radium and of thorium. The last, written by Rutherford and Soddy under the simple title "Radioactive Change," was a striking and masterly review of their work over the last few years. Extracts will be quoted now, some of them in skeleton form, to show some of their lines of thought and argument:

"All cases of radioactive change that have been studied can be resolved into the production of one substance by another . . . when several changes occur together they are not simultaneous but successive. Thus thorium produces thorium X, the thorium X produces the thorium emanation, and the latter produces the excited activity."

"Both the radioactivity and the emanating power of thorium X decay according to the same law and *at the same rate* . . . Hence it is not possible to regard radioactivity as the *consequence* of changes that have already taken place. The rays emitted must be an *accompaniment* of the change of the radiating system into the next one produced."

"There is every reason to suppose not merely that the expulsion of a charged particle accompanies the change, but that this expulsion actually *is* the change."

After pointing out that the alphas from all substances differ only to a slight extent in penetrating power, and going on to give some numbers taken from their paper on "deviability," Rutherford and Soddy say:

Ernest Rutherford in about 1904.

E. Rutherford. 1904

"There are thus strong reasons for the belief that the α-rays generally are projections,* and that the mass of the particle is of the same order as that of the hydrogen atom and very large compared with . . . the β or easily deviable ray from the same element.

"With regard to the part played in radioactivity by the two types of radiation, there can be no doubt that the α-rays are by far the more important."

Rutherford believed this firmly, because the α-rays carried much more energy than the β-rays, and it was mainly with α-rays that he worked for the rest of his life. Had he chosen β-rays, he would certainly not have discovered the atomic nucleus.

"The complexity of the phenomena of radioactivity is due to the existence as a general rule of several different types of matter changing at the same time into one another, each type possessing a different radioactive constant.

"The law of radioactive change, that the rate of change is proportional to the quantity of changing substance, is also the law of monomolecular chemical reaction. Radioactive change, therefore, must be of such a kind as to involve one system only."

Without taking space to explain the laws of chemical reactions, the comment is worth while that Soddy was a chemist and that other chemists had to be persuaded that their beliefs were being undermined in one respect only; that not all atoms go on unchanged for ever. There are several other passages emphasizing that, apart from the peculiarities of behaviour in precipitation, etc., of extremely small amounts of matter, radioactive elements are chemically quite normal. This is perhaps the place to add that an alpha-disintegration moves the element two places towards the beginning of the periodic table, and that a beta-disintegration moves it one place in the opposite direction. That was established

* Nowadays, the word "projectiles" would be used.

from the chemical behaviour of the radioactive elements, and Soddy took a leading part in recognizing that there was some such connection between the type of radioactive change and the chemistry of the "mother" and "daughter" elements. It was he who coined the word "isotopes" (Greek: same place) for atoms with different physical properties that are chemically inseparable.

This famous 1903 paper ends with some calculations about the energy released in radioactive change: "At least twenty thousand times, and may be a million times, as great as the energy of any molecular change ... The maintenance of solar energy, for example, no longer presents any fundamental difficulty if the internal energy of the component elements is considered to be available."

These are impressive words, particularly now that we know the sun's energy is derived from nuclear reactions, though not among the heavier elements which Rutherford and Soddy had in mind and which are the present source of man-made nuclear power. Incidentally, Rutherford and Soddy mention the possibility of elements heavier than uranium, and that they too will be radioactive. It was nearly half a century before such elements were in fact discovered.

Nobody who has read this paper of Rutherford and Soddy's can fail to be amazed that so many truths were extracted in so short a time from such a complicated situation, many details of which had still to be understood. Compare, for example, their 1903 list of the thorium "family" (Fig. 8) with the one given by Rutherford, Chadwick and Ellis in their book *Radiations from Radioactive Substances* published in 1930. (Fig. 9).

Just as Darwin produced many lines of argument for the evolution of plants and animals by natural selection, so Rutherford and Soddy had, as we have seen, many reasons to give for abandoning the belief that atoms were all unchangeable. In their case, the

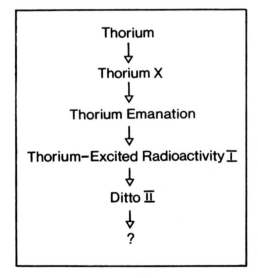

Fig. 8

NUCLIDE	ATOMIC WEIGHT	Z	TYPE OF RADIATION	HALF-LIFE	
Thorium Th	232.12	90	α	1.65 x 10^{10} years	α
Mesothorium 1 Ms Th 1	(228)	88	ß	6.7 years	ß
Mesothorium 2 Ms Th 2	(228)	89	ß	6.13 years	ß
Radiothorium Rd Th	(228)	90	α	1.90 years	α
Thorium X Th X	(224)	88	α	3.64 days	α
Thoron Tn	(220)	86	α	54.5 sec.	α
Thorium A Th A	(216)	84	α	0 145 sec.	α
Thorium B Th B	(212)	82	ß	10.6 hours	ß
Thorium C Th C	(212)	83	αß	60.5 min.	35% / 65%
Thorium C' Th C'	(212)	84	α	ca. 10^{-11} sec. (?)	α / ß
Thorium C" Th C"	(208)	81	ß	3.20 min.	ß / α
Thorium D Th D	207.77	82	Stable	—	

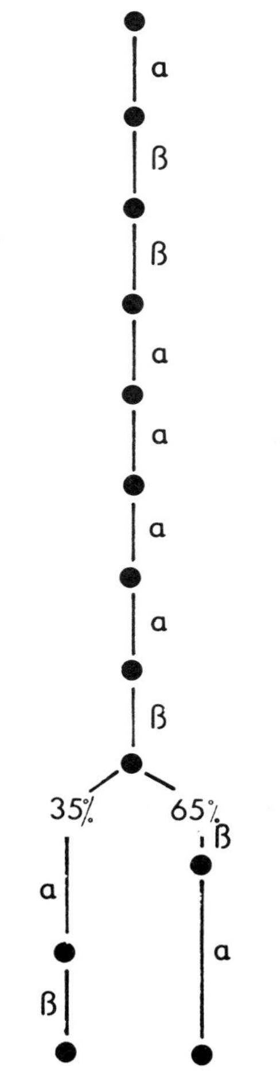

Fig. 9

scientific world was convinced much more rapidly, and it was the 1903 papers that did it.

Their skilful presentation of the transformation of atoms to the chemists worked well, but Rutherford had more trouble in convincing some of his fellow physicists, particularly about the great energy released in radioactive processes. Lord Kelvin at first

Sir William Thomson, Lord Kelvin (1824–1907), British physicist who made important advances in the science of thermodynamics. One of his earliest papers dealt with the age of the earth and led him into a long argument with biologists and geologists. He also invented a number of telegraphic and scientific instruments.

refused to believe that atoms could be storehouses of so much energy and suggested that it was supplied to them by "etherial waves."

Other physicists, however, saw that the energy of radioactivity, released within the Earth over many millions of years, could settle a controversy between Kelvin and the biologists—in favour of the biologists. If there had been no source of heat *within* the Earth, it would have cooled from its molten state to its present temperature in a time that Kelvin, an expert on heat, estimated to be less than 40 million years, and only in the later part of that time would life have been possible. Darwin, on the other hand, had believed a time of 300 million years or more to be needed for the evolution of today's plants and animals. It is radioactive heat that has made the cooling so much slower. Kelvin gracefully gave way.

5 *Alpha-particles and the Atomic Nucleus*

"I know what atoms look like."

Rutherford.

So far, the least penetrating radiation from radioactive substances has been called "alpha-rays." This was Rutherford's name, but the title of alpha-*particles* for this chapter has been chosen deliberately, not just because it has been commonly used by physicists over the last half-century, but because the chapter is concerned with Rutherford's proof that they are indeed particles and with his use of them, as *individual particles,* to discover how atoms are structured. It is true that in modern physics the distinction between waves and particles is not very sharp, but it is usually sharp enough for practical purposes.

The first step towards recognizing that "α-rays" are in fact individual ions of helium was the insistence of Rutherford and Soddy that each α-ray was emitted at the time its parent atom transformed itself into a different atom. If we write,

$$\text{Radium} \rightarrow \text{Radon} + \alpha$$

we are not just writing a statement about the behaviour of radium in bulk, but about what happens to a single atom of radium.

The second step, the subject of one of the 1903 papers, was an experiment that was simple in principle but difficult with the techniques of the time.

X-rays, α-, β- and γ-rays had all been tried for magnetic and electric deflection, and only β-rays had shown any large effect; they are, in fact, fast-moving electrons. Pierre Curie had found a very small deflection of α-rays in the opposite direction. Rutherford decided to use the strongest available fields and very narrow beams of α-rays, detecting the alphas by their ionization. A diagram of the apparatus is shown in

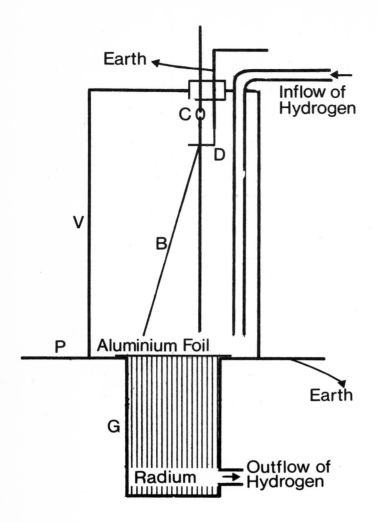

Earth

C O

D

V

B

P   Aluminium Foil

Inflow of
Hydrogen

Earth

G

Radium

Outflow of
Hydrogen

Fig. 10 Apparatus used by Rutherford
to deflect α-rays.

Fig. 10. It was filled with hydrogen gas, in which the α-rays travel further than they would in air, so that most of their ionization was produced near the electroscope and not in the gaps between the metal plates. Also, β- and γ-rays give *less* ionization in hydrogen than in air, so they interfered less with Rutherford's measurements. Fig. 11 shows how the experiment worked; without any field to bend their paths, more α-rays can pass through the gaps between the plates than when a field is applied. A magnetic field, perpen-

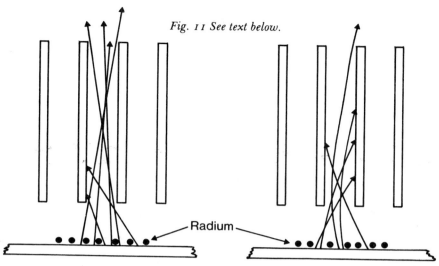

Fig. 11 See text below.

Radium

Radium

Fig. 12	Rate of discharge of electroscope in volts per minute
(1) Without magnetic field.............................	8.33
(2) With magnetic field	1.72
(3) Radium covered with thin layer of mica to absorb all α-rays....................................	0.93
(4) Radium covered with mica and magnetic field applied...	0.92

dicular to the plane of the paper, was applied from outside the apparatus by an electromagnet; when an electric field was wanted, alternate plates were connected to the positive and negative terminals of a battery of small accumulators, giving up to 600 volts. Rutherford said that he used to test the voltage of his batteries by putting his hands across them; I doubt whether he did this with the full 600 volts!

Fig. 12 shows a typical set of results for the magnetic field; with the electric field the effects were smaller.

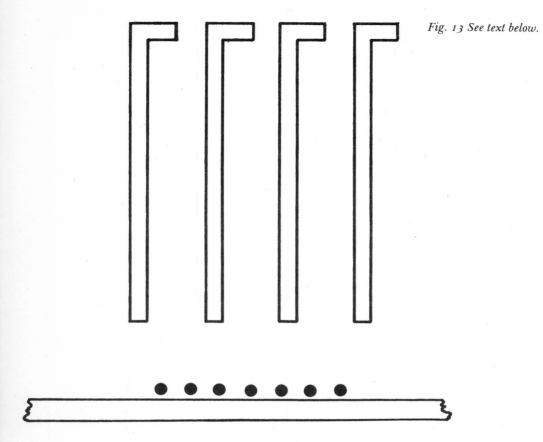

Fig. 13 See text below.

The direction of deflection was found by covering half of each slit with a brass strip (Fig. 13) and seeing what difference to the electroscope reading was made by reversing the direction of the magnetic field. It showed that the α-rays were positively charged. By comparing the effects of the electric and magnetic fields, somewhat as Thomson had done for electrons and for positive ions from his discharge-tubes, Rutherford estimated that their charge-to-mass ratio was within about 30% of what would be expected for a singly-charged ion of mass 2 or a doubly-charged ion of mass 4. He also calculated that the α-rays from radium were travelling at about 25,000 kilometres a second, which is roughly a tenth of the speed of light.

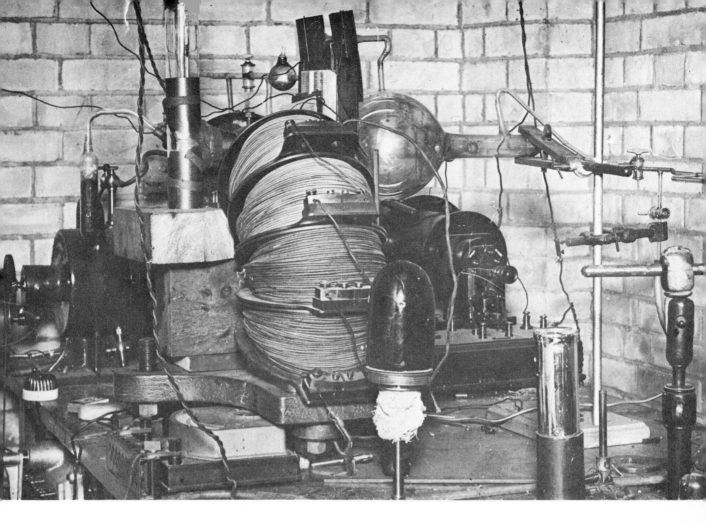

J. J. Thomson's apparatus for measuring the charge-to-mass ratio of positive and negative ions.

Now helium gas is always found in association with radioactive minerals and it had been suggested that helium might be a product of radioactive transformation. Rutherford therefore concluded that α-rays were most probably doubly-charged helium atoms. This conclusion was reached in 1903 but, over the years, Rutherford and his students made increasingly accurate measurements, as did other physicists. By 1906 the e/m value had been found to agree with the He^{++} hypothesis to about 5%, and later experiments improved the agreement.

A very elegant experiment was done by Rutherford and Royds to show that α-rays, when they are brought to rest by passing through matter, end up as neutral helium atoms. They left radon gas to decay in a glass tube with walls so thin that α-rays could penetrate them. This "α-ray tube," marked *A* in Fig. 14, was enclosed in another glass envelope connected to a small discharge-tube, *V*, into which gas appearing in the outer vessel could be compressed. The discharge showed the characteristic optical spectrum of helium.

The amount of radon obtainable at any one time from as much as a gram of radium gives only about a tenth of a microgram of helium; less than a cubic millimetre of the gas at atmospheric pressure. Most of this helium remains embedded in the glass walls of the outer tube *T*, so Rutherford and Royds were working with extremely small amounts, and such an experiment shows how very sensitive a spectroscopic test can be. It is also very reliable; not only the pattern of lines but the actual wavelength of each line is different for every chemical element.

The availability of beams of α-particles of definite velocity was of great importance for much of Rutherford's later work, particularly for exploring the structure of atoms; still more important was the development of ways of observing and counting single α-particles. Only one of these, the scintillation counter, will be described here; Rutherford did not invent it, and indeed he clung rather long to a much less simple electrical counter that he and H. Geiger did invent,[*] but scintillations were the essential tool of the greatest discoveries of his Manchester period, and widely used until the 1920's and occasionally in the 1930's—for example by Cockcroft and Walton in their disintegration of lithium by protons.

Various substances, notably zinc sulphide, emit visible light when exposed to radioactive substances. In 1903, Crookes and two German physicists had independently noticed that when the radiation was weak and the observer's eye had become sensitive by having been in the dark for some time, the light was not steady. A low-power microscope shows that the

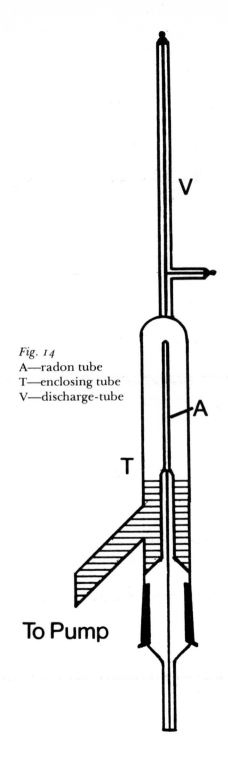

Fig. 14
A—radon tube
T—enclosing tube
V—discharge-tube

[*] The forerunner of the "Geiger counter" more accurately called the "Geiger-Müller counter."

Rutherford with Hans Wilhelm Geiger (1882–1945) who invented, between 1908 and 1913, a simple device for counting alpha-particles one by one.

fluctuations are because the light comes in individual flashes. It soon became clear that these are due to the impact of α-particles, and Crookes saw that this was a marvellously simple way of "looking" at them.

Rutherford adopted this suggestion in his first book on radioactivity (1904):

"In the scintillations of zinc sulphide, we are actually witnessing the effect produced by the impact on the screen of single atoms of matter projected with enormous velocity." His enthusiasm for scintillations as showing the impact of single α-particles was accompanied by doubts as to whether every particle caused a scintillation. If not, the method could not confidently be used for quantitative measurements, and Rutherford did not use it until it had been verified that the number of scintillations agreed with the

63

number of α-particles registered by the Rutherford–Geiger electrical counter.

Rutherford's greatest discovery, the nuclear structure of atoms, was achieved by using his favourite particles, the alphas, and the scintillation counter. Like so many of his earlier successes, it resulted from a series of careful investigations of what at first must have seemed a complicated matter. As early as 1906, while deflecting α-rays by a magnetic field, Rutherford had noticed that if some air was left in the apparatus, the well-collimated beam became spread over a perceptible range of angles. Passage through a very thin foil gave a similar result; for example, a sheet of mica three hundredths of a millimetre thick gave deflections of two degrees or more. Now to change the direction by this amount in so short a distance would require forces very much greater than those given by electric or magnetic fields that can be obtained in the ordinary way—10,000 volts per centimetre was Rutherford's estimate, even if the field were in the same direction throughout the thickness of the mica. Such strong fields certainly do not exist in bulk materials; so if the deflections are of an electrical origin, they must occur *within* the atoms, and the fields must be of greater strength still.

Now, whatever the inner structure of atoms may be, they certainly contain electrons, negatively-charged, and there must be equal amounts of positive charge in them to make the atom electrically neutral. The α-particle carries a positive charge and will be attracted by the electrons and repelled by the positive charges. So if it passes just to the right of an electron it will be deflected slightly to the left and if it passes to the right of a positive charge it will be deflected to the right. Such a "collision" with an electron can deflect an α-ray by only an extremely small amount, for the electron is about 10,000 times lighter than the alpha; a golf-ball cannot be deflected much by hitting a fly. The positive charges, if attached to the more massive

Probably Rutherford's first car, acquired when he was at Manchester.

parts of the atom, might give bigger deflections, and thousands of very small deflections in random directions—right and left, up and down—could build up to a sizable total.

The theory of this "multiple scattering" can be worked out by statistical methods, even if the details of each scattering collision are not known: for example, the average angle of resultant deflection increases in proportion to the square root of the number of collisions (i.e. in proportion to the square root of thickness of the scattering foil). Moreover one can predict in which way the number of scatterings by a multiple process will fall off with increasing angle of scattering. Geiger and Marsden found an increase of average scattering angle with foil thickness, just about as predicted, and for small angles of scattering the angular distribution was also about right; but at larger angles, though the number of scattered particles continued to decrease, it was greater than corresponded to the theory as verified for small angles. Indeed a few particles were deflected by more than 90° and could be observed coming out of the front, not of the back, of the foil.

This was in 1909, and speaking in Winnipeg that summer, Rutherford said, "The conclusion is unavoidable that the atom is the seat of an intense electric field, for otherwise it would be impossible to change the direction of the particle over such a minute distance as the diameter of the molecule*." The last words are particularly interesting. They show that Rutherford regarded the large-angle scatterings as the result of single encounters, in contrast to the statistical build-up of very small deflections which could account for the small-angle scattering; they also suggest that his thoughts were not yet with any more localized centre of force than the atom as the whole; and they show his acceptance of the general belief that the forces acting within atoms were electrical.

* "Molecule" was almost certainly a slip, for Geiger and Marsden had been using foils of metallic elements, not compounds.

Rutherford did not commit himself further for about a year. In December 1910, Geiger has written, "He came into my room, obviously in the best of tempers, and told me that now he knew what the atom looked like and what the strong scatterings signified." He had come to the idea that the positive charge of the atom, together with most of its mass, lay in a nucleus much smaller than the atom as a whole; if this were true for heavy atoms, such as those of Geiger and Marsden's gold foils, then presumably an α-particle was a helium nucleus.

Rutherford was a good practical mathematician and had in earlier years interested himself in Newton's calculations of the orbits of planets round the sun, with an attractive force varying as the inverse square of the distance. He now made calculations of the orbits corresponding to an inverse-square (repulsive) electrostatic force between the helium nucleus and the nucleus of the atom which was doing the scattering. He worked out, among other things, how many α-particles should be scattered in various directions, and saw that this would be a very effective test of his theory. Geiger returned to detailed measurements of the large-angle scattering and found excellent agreement. Fig. 15 shows typical orbits and Fig. 16 represents, in very diagrammatic form, Geiger and Marsden's experimental arrangement.

Manuscript notes remain to show that the nuclear atom was not just a sudden inspiration. Rutherford approached the mathematical problem in various ways, initially using the radius of the whole atom as one of the factors in the calculation. In the end, realizing that the large-angle scatterings must happen exceedingly close to the centre on the atomic scale of distances, he discarded the atom as such entirely and emerged with a somewhat long but essentially straightforward calculation for the bare nucleus.

Now the *relative* numbers of α-rays scattered in

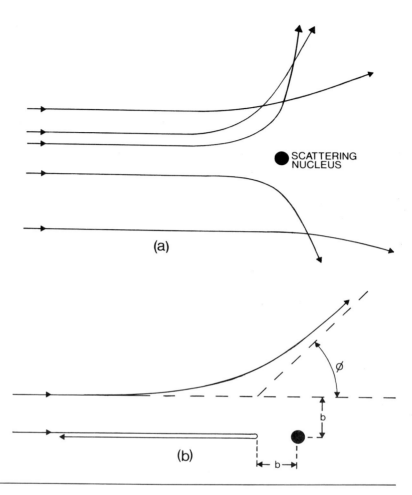

Fig. 15 (a) Orbits of α-rays near a nucleus; (b) shows what is meant by the "angle of scattering," φ, and the closest distance for head-on approach, b.

SCATTERING NUCLEUS

(a)

(b)

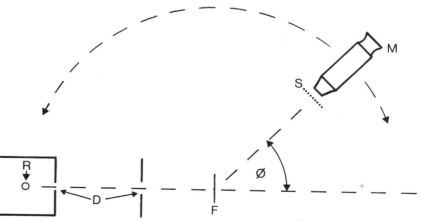

Fig. 16 R—thin-walled glass tube filled with radon, seen end-on; D—diaphragms (small holes or narrow slits) to make the α-rays into a narrow beam; S—scintillation screen; M—microscope focussed on screen.
S and M are rotated together about F to various angles (φ).

different directions do not, according to Rutherford's theory, depend on anything but the inverse-square law of force between the nuclei; not even on the velocities of the particles, nor even on classical mechanics; the quantum theory calculation, done much later, gives the same angular distribution. This was quite remarkably good fortune, but then fortune does sometimes favour the brave.

The *actual* number scattered at any angle does, of course, depend on many factors, including obvious ones such as the number of incident particles and the number of scattering nuclei in unit area of the foil. In particular, it depends on the number of unit charges carried by each scattering nucleus, and this came out to be very roughly half the atomic weight of the element concerned. A little later, Van den Broek suggested that the nuclear charge might be Ze, with Z being the "atomic number" of the element, i.e. the number of its place in the periodic table, and e the unit charge—i.e. the charge on a proton. Much later (1920) Chadwick confirmed this by experiments similar in principle to those of Geiger and Marsden, but designed to give optimum counting rates both of the scattered particles and of a known small fraction of the incident beam. In the meantime, Moseley's work on the X-ray spectra of different elements had virtually settled the matter, as described on page 72.

The Solvay Physics Conference on "Theories of Radiation" at Brussels in 1911.

GOLDSCHMIDT   PLANCK
NERNST   BRILLOUIN

LINDEMANN   HASENOHRL
ERFELD   DE BROGLIE   HOSTELET
LORENTZ   KNUDSEN   HERZEN   JEANS   RUTHERFORD
          WARBURG   WIEN
          PERRIN   Mme CURIE   POINCARÉ   KAMERLINGH ONNES   EINSTEIN   LANGEVIN

The agreement between experiment and theory also gives confidence in the fundamental assumption of inverse-square repulsion, but how close to the centre of the nucleus did this law continue to hold? The experiment had tested it down to the closest distance of approach (*b,* in Fig. 15) for the largest scattering angles, which was in fact about 10^{-11}cm. (10^{-13}m.). Later measurements pushed the limit, for gold, to about 3×10^{-12}cm. (3×10^{-14}m.).

At short enough distances, however, the inverse-square law must fail; the nucleus cannot be a mathematical point or the electrostatic energy of its charge would be infinite; so if the α-ray passes through the actual volume of the nucleus, the force (and therefore the angle of scattering) will be less than for the "point" nucleus of Rutherford's calculation.

It turns out that with the α-particles' limited kinetic energies (and the fastest available ones were already used in these experiments) the best chance of "getting into the nucleus" is with lighter target elements; their smaller nuclear charge more than compensates for their presumably smaller size. Experiments by Bieler and by Rutherford and Chadwick showed some deviation from "inverse-square" theory for alphas that approached closer than about 10^{-14}m. to the centre of aluminium nuclei. Much later measurements of nuclear radii by quite different methods have shown that they are roughly proportional to the cube root of the nuclear mass, so the density of nuclear mass is nearly constant. It is more than 10^{15} times that of water.

Niels Bohr (1885–1962), the Danish nuclear physicist who used Max Planck's "Quantum theory" and Rutherford's discovery of the nucleus to provide a theoretical picture of the atom.

6 Inside the Atom and its Nucleus

"Here we are on Tom Tiddler's ground, picking up gold and silver."

Traditional.

This chapter deals with the effects of Rutherford's discoveries upon the understanding of what are the "parts" of atoms and of their nuclei, and of how these parts fit together.

The parts of *atoms* were settled conclusively by the discovery of the nucleus; the rest of the atom, roughly ten thousand times larger in diameter and thus 10^{12} times in volume, was obviously occupied by electrons. In a neutral atom, the number of negative electrons must be equal to the number of positive unit charges of the nucleus. What was this number for each particular kind of atom? It was pretty certainly *one* for hydrogen and *two* for helium, for hydrogen positive ions had never been found with more than one unit charge, or helium ions with more than two. As we have seen, it had been suggested that this relation continued through the periodic table, the "Z"th element having Z electrons and a nuclear charge Ze.

As far back as 1900, Max Planck in Germany had made a discovery that ranks alongside Einstein's theory of relativity, for together they radically changed theoretical physics. Planck's quantum theory was not mentioned in Chapter 2 because it had no effect on the understanding of atoms until 1913. Then, Niels Bohr, a young Dane who worked for a year in Rutherford's department in Manchester developed it in combination with the nuclear picture of atoms. His theory involved orbits of electrons round the nucleus, like planets round the sun. He calculated the frequencies of lines in the optical spectrum of atomic hydrogen—the simplest of all atomic structures—and found remarkable agreement with the observed spectrum. Now Bohr could extend his calculation, at least roughly, to atoms with more than one electron. By the time the number of electrons (and therefore the number of unit charges on the nucleus) had risen to about twenty, the frequencies were so high that the lines associated with the inner-most orbits had moved from the visible range, through the ultra-violet, into the X-ray region.

What would be expected on his calculations was a quite simple pattern of X-ray lines, exactly repeated at higher frequencies on going from one element to the next. The pattern is simple because the electrons group themselves into what are called "shells."

H. J. J. Moseley, also in Rutherford's laboratory, now measured the X-ray spectra of many elements and found just such a regularity, and from then on there was never any doubt that the Zth element had Z nuclear charges and Z electrons. We call Z the *atomic number* of the element.

Atoms of a given chemical element (defined by Z, for chemistry depends on the electrons) can have nuclei of different masses, and these masses are very nearly whole numbers if a suitable scale of mass is used, for example ordinary oxygen being the standard at 16·000. On that scale, all atoms have whole-number masses to about 1%, and the number for each of them is called its *mass-number, A*. Atoms (or nuclei) with the same Z but different A are called *isotopes* of the element in question, and the nucleus of any particular atomic type, having a particular Z and a particular A, is called a *nuclide*. Thus the nuclides symbolized by $^{63}_{29}$Cu and $^{65}_{29}$Cu are isotopes of copper, the 29th element, with mass-numbers 63 and 65.

That being settled, the question is what are the building-bricks of nuclei? Since the masses of electrons are almost negligible, the simplest assumption was that all nuclei are built of protons and electrons; $^{63}_{29}$Cu, for example, having 63 protons and 34 elec-

Rutherford's research room at the Cavendish Laboratory, Cambridge.

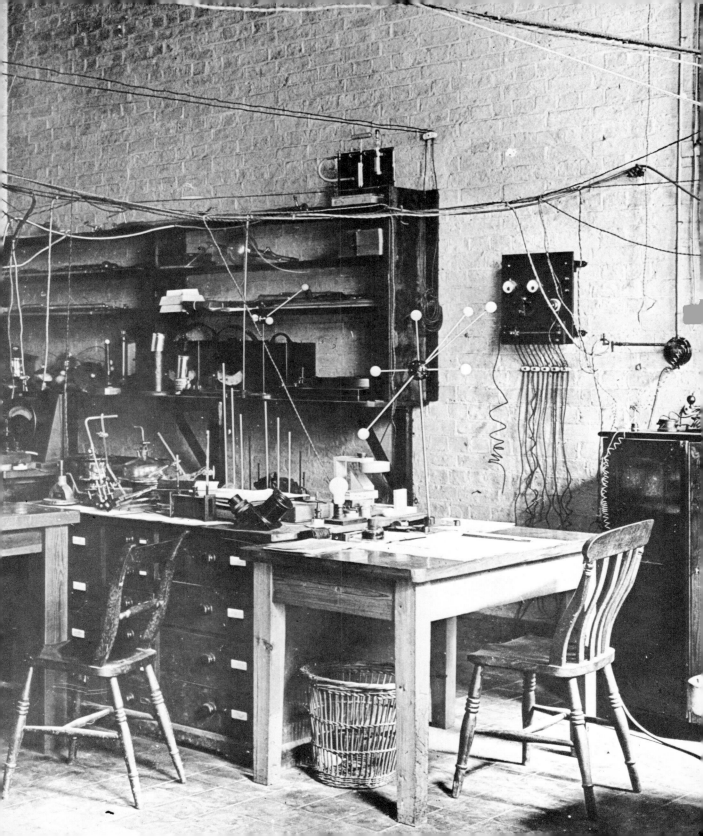

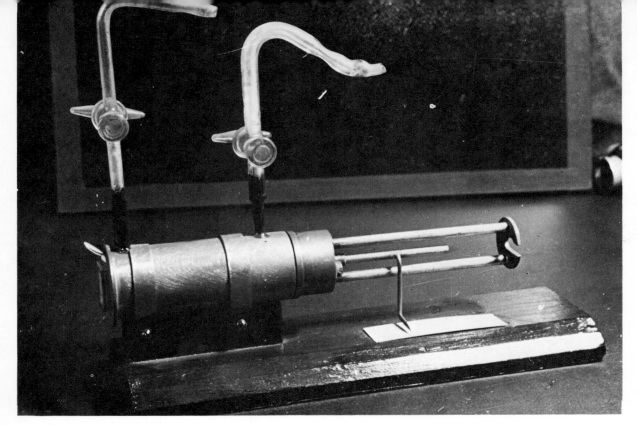

trons. There were difficulties about this, the simplest being that quantum theory says that electrons are too big to fit into nuclei.

At this stage, we must leave this problem and go on to another of Rutherford's discoveries, the splitting of nuclei by bombarding them with α-particles.

Marsden, in 1914, had found that if α-particles were passed through hydrogen gas towards a zinc sulphide screen, scintillations were observed at distances far beyond the range of the α-particles. They were due to hydrogen nuclei—protons—knocked forwards by the impact of the alphas; a quite elementary calculation, using the principle of the conservation of kinetic energy and of momentum, shows that in a head-on collision the proton, having 1/4 the mass of the helium nucleus, will be given 8/5 of its velocity; and at a given velocity a proton has much the same range as an α-particle. The proton scintillations, though faint, could be reliably counted, and Rutherford studied

The first artifical transmutation of nuclei. Rutherford's apparatus for bombarding gases with alpha-particles.

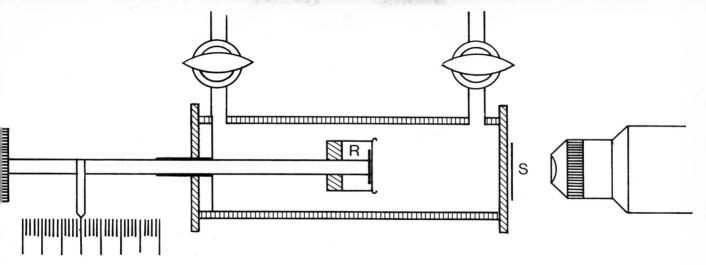

Fig. 17 R—disc covered with radium B
and radium C;
S—scintillation screen.

these He-H collisions in detail, verifying by magnetic and electric deflections that the knocked-on particles indeed had the charge-to-mass ratio of protons.

The great discovery came after the end of the First World War, in 1919. Then, using the same apparatus (Fig. 17) that he had used for the hydrogen collisions, Rutherford passed α-particles into heavier gases. "Knocked-on" nuclei would then have ranges less than that of the alphas; but in the case of nitrogen, but not with oxygen or carbon dioxide, he observed scintillations at long range. These he identified as protons, ejected from the nitrogen nucleus; he was observing the first artificial disintegration of nuclei, the process being represented by $^{14}_{7}N + {}^{4}_{2}He \rightarrow {}^{17}_{8}O + {}^{1}_{1}H$.

Soon after finishing this experiment, Rutherford moved to Cambridge as Cavendish Professor, bringing with him not only much of his Manchester apparatus and radium, but also his young colleague J. Chadwick. He was able to continue his own experiments as well as to start many research students working on problems in what may now fairly be called "nuclear physics." Most of these were on topics where it was fairly certain that useful if not important results could be obtained; some were longer-term projects and some extended beyond the use of his favourite α-rays.

A few of the many successes of his Cambridge staff and students will be mentioned shortly, but I will quote now some passages from a lecture he gave to the Royal Society in 1920. They show him as a prophet of particles that had not then been discovered, but basing his prophecies on an experimental result that was wrong! In addition to the long-range scintillations from the disintegration of nitrogen, he had seen rather brighter scintillations that stopped at a range of 9 cm., a little beyond the range of the alphas that were causing the nitrogen disintegrations. From magnetic deflection experiments, he concluded that the 9 cm. particles were helium nuclei of mass 3. Using the accepted proton–electron composition of nuclei, he went on to say:

"From the analogy with helium we may expect the nucleus of the new atom to consist of three H nuclei and one electron . . . If we are correct in this assumption it seems very likely that one electron can also bind two H nuclei and possibly also one H nucleus. In the one case, this entails the possible existence of an atom of mass nearly 2 carrying one charge, which is to be regarded as an isotope of hydrogen. In the other case, it involves the idea of an atom of mass 1 which has zero nucleus charge. Such an atomic structure is by no means impossible . . . Its external field would be zero, except very close to the nucleus, and in consequence it would be able to move freely through matter . . . it should readily enter the structure of atoms and may either unite with the nucleus or be disintegrated by its intense field, resulting possibly in the escape of a charged H atom or an electron or both."

From the "ifs" and "possiblys" in these sentences, it is clear that Rutherford did not feel quite as sure of himself as usual; yet he had predicted ^{3}He, which turned up many years later as a stable isotope of ordinary ^{4}He, and had gone on to predict ^{2}H (deuterium) and also the existence, and several of the remarkable properties of neutrons.

A year later, he made further experiments and

Sir James Chadwick (1891–   ),
English physicist whose discovery of
the neutron won him the 1935 Nobel
Prize for Physics.

found that the 9 cm. scintillations were due to higher energy α-particles, ordinary ⁴He, emitted by the source and not produced in the gas. It is better not to be wrong, but better to find that out for yourself than to wait for someone else to put you right.

One of the experiments to test for the existence of neutrons was done at Rutherford's suggestion by J. H. Roberts, who measured very accurately the heat developed in a discharge-tube, shielded to prevent the escape of light or X-rays, and compared it with the electrical energy supplied to the tube. Particles "able to move freely through matter" would have carried energy with them, but no difference between the electrical input and the heat output was found.

Nevertheless, Rutherford did not give up thinking about neutrons, and their actual discovery in his laboratory by his friend Chadwick gave him great pleasure. Like Rutherford himself in the early days of radioactivity, Chadwick resolved a puzzling situation by a simple solution that could be checked by further experiments. Without going into details, it is enough to say neutrons were first obtained by bombarding the element beryllium with α-particles and had previously been mistaken for γ-rays.

As soon as the neutron had been discovered, the composition of nuclei became clear; they are made of neutrons and protons, and our example of $^{63}_{29}$Cu contains 29 protons and 34 neutrons. Rutherford had been talking about the nucleus as "Tom Tiddler's ground" where gold and silver were to be picked up; Chadwick had certainly struck gold.

It may seem strange that, although Chadwick and other members of the Cavendish Laboratory did experiments with neutrons immediately afterwards, Rutherford's prediction about their ability to enter nuclei was not fully exploited there. The simplest of all reasons is probably the best: nuclear physics was spreading all over the world and no one laboratory could do everything or even expect a large share of

new discoveries. The transmutation of nuclei by very slow neutrons was a triumph of E. Fermi, an already distinguished theoretical physicist who turned to experiments and, during the Second World War, built the first nuclear reactor.

To close this short chapter, a rough picture of "what nuclei look like" to modern eyes may be useful. They are, as we have seen, assemblies of protons and neutrons; the protons repel one another electrically, but this repulsion is overcome by attractive forces of a kind that cannot be understood in terms of ordinary mechanics or of electricity. These forces are due to the continual exchange of sub-nuclear particles, called π-mesons, between protons and neutrons.

Nuclei as a whole are more or less spherical. Some of them have what is called "spin," a word put in inverted commas because although they have what in mechanics is called "angular momentum" and may be slightly flattened like the Earth, it is not a simple rotation of the nucleus. The heaviest nuclei are distorted from the shape of a sphere towards that of a Rugby football; this is because of the repulsion of their many protons. Such nuclei, by themselves or under bombardment, can separate into two: the process of *fission*.

As for the inner structure of nuclei, all that can be said here is that, just as the various electrons in an atom can be grouped into "shells," so can the protons, and the neutrons, in a complex nucleus be grouped. In each case, we must beware of thinking of them as like the layers of an onion; for atoms it can safely be said that electrons belonging to different shells are at different average distances from the nucleus, but for nuclei no safe geometrical explanation can be given. We must be grateful that there is still so much to be learned about nuclei, and particularly grateful that they are so very much smaller than atoms; otherwise, the problem of *atomic* structure might have defeated even Rutherford.

Rutherford with Professor Sir J. J. Thomson in about 1935.

The original "cloud-chamber" used
by C. T. R. Wilson in which particles far
too small to be seen made visible
tracks.

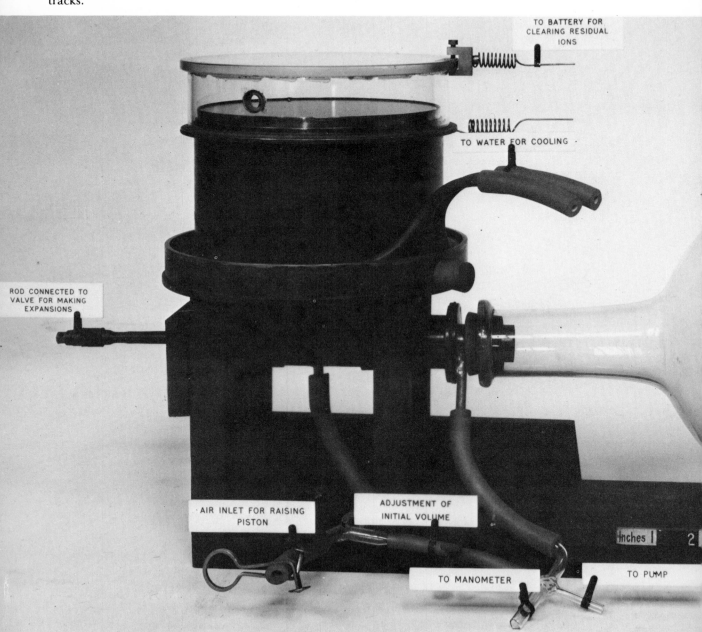

TO BATTERY FOR
CLEARING RESIDUAL
IONS

TO WATER FOR COOLING

ROD CONNECTED TO
VALVE FOR MAKING
EXPANSIONS

AIR INLET FOR RAISING
PISTON

ADJUSTMENT OF
INITIAL VOLUME

Inches 1   2

TO MANOMETER

TO PUMP

7 Rutherford and Modern Nuclear Physics

"It is as easy to count atomies as to resolve the propositions of a lover."

Shakespeare.

Though most of Rutherford's own discoveries had been made using ionization chambers or scintillation counters, he was alive to the need for better ways of counting nuclear particles and of measuring their energies.

One of these, the cloud-chamber of C. T. R. Wilson, was invented in Cambridge and Rutherford took a friendly interest in its development, but its origin had nothing to do with nuclear physics. Wilson was interested in how clouds are formed in the atmosphere. The droplets of water condense upon particles of dust; if there is no dust they condense, though much less readily, on the ions that are produced by the sun's ultra-violet radiation.

Cooling moist air by suddenly expanding its volume, Wilson had established these facts, so important to meteorology; he went on to use his cloud-chamber to make visible the tracks of ionizing particles, such as α-particles. Droplets will condense along the line of ions left by a particle that has passed through the gas just before the expansion, and if a flash of light is provided just after the expansion, the track can be photographed.

Rutherford took a much more direct interest in another technique which, for a good many years, was a replacement of the scintillation counter, and indeed was a great improvement. Greinacher in Switzerland had coupled an amplifier to an ionization chamber and observed the pulses of ionization current from single α-particles, and Rutherford encouraged two of his students, C. E. Wynn-Williams and F. A. B. Ward, to develop this discovery.

In a few years (by the early 1930s), it was possible to count α-particles rapidly and automatically. More than that, the amount of electric charge passing to the amplifier is proportional to the number of ions made by the particle in the chamber; so if the whole of its track lies within the chamber the energy of each particle can be recorded. In practice, it is often more convenient to admit particles through a thin "window" into the chamber, accepting a known loss of energy. The window, however, would vibrate when sounds reached it or if the apparatus was knocked, or if anyone passed with a heavy tread. The valves in the amplifier were also "microphonic." Rutherford found it difficult to keep quiet enough, and his entry to the room was a frequent problem, for he had to pass through it to get to his private laboratory.

Such a "pulse ionization chamber" was used by Chadwick in his discovery of neutrons.

At about the same time, physicists in various laboratories were working on ways of replacing natural sources of fast-moving nuclei by artificial ones. Starting with ions from a discharge-tube, enormously greater numbers of particles could be put into a narrow beam, and the kind of particle was open to choice; H^+ ions (protons) were obviously very desirable projectiles for disintegration experiments like those that Rutherford had done using natural α-rays. The difficulty was that to match the kinetic energy of a typical α-particle, several million volts would need to be applied to the ion beam.

Ways of applying smaller voltages many times in succession to the travelling ions were invented, and among these the cyclotron of Lawrence and Livingston (1930) is justly famous, but before it had been applied to actual nuclear physics Cockcroft and Walton (1932) achieved the first transmutation by artificially accelerated particles, with less than half a million volts.

Rutherford in the Cavendish Laboratory in the 1930s below a large illuminated sign: "Talk Softly Please." He is talking to J. A. Ratcliffe who later became Director of the Radio Research Station at Slough, Middlesex.

The story of the start of their work is best told by an extract from Cockcroft's lecture given in Stockholm when he and Walton received Nobel Prizes for their achievements:

"I began this work in the Cavendish Laboratory under the direction of Lord RUTHERFORD in 1928. At this time experimental work on the energies of α-particles ejected from the radioactive elements had shown that these particles could have a substantially lower energy than the calculated height of the potential barrier around the nucleus. For a time this was somewhat of a puzzle, but in 1928 GAMOW, who was then working in Copenhagen, and also GURNEY and CONDON, showed that this could be readily explained by attributing wave properties to the escaping α-particle so that the particle could escape from the nucleus without having a high enough energy to surmount the potential barrier. GAMOW visited the Cavendish Laboratory in 1928 and I discussed with him the converse problem—the energy which would be required for a proton accelerated by high voltages to penetrate the nuclei of the light elements. As a result of these talks I prepared a memorandum which I sent to RUTHERFORD showing that there was a quite high probability for the Boron nucleus to be penetrated by a proton of only 300 kilovolts energy whilst conditions for Lithium were even more favourable. RUTHERFORD then agreed to my beginning work on this problem and I was soon joined by Dr. WALTON who had previously been working on the development of an early linear accelerator and also on an equally early betatron."

The project was a landmark in Rutherford's still-developing scientific character, for he backed it on the basis of a purely theoretical prediction. For many years, he had spoken of theorists as though they were competitors and not colleagues: "The theorists are on their hindlegs and it is up to us to get them down again" or "How can a fellow sit down at a table and calculate something that would take me, me, six months to measure in the laboratory?" Sir Nevill Mott, one of Rutherford's successors as Cavendish Professor, has written that Rutherford was far too great a man not to see that theory and experiment must intermingle to give a true view of nature; now, in his late fifties, he was ready to lay out a good deal of money in that spirit.

The apparatus built by Cockcroft and Walton was based on a high-voltage transformer made in the Trafford Park works of the Metropolitan-Vickers Company in Manchester, where Cockcroft had earlier been one of the research staff. A voltage-multiplying circuit was used, and the resulting voltage appeared across the top and bottom terminals of a stack of glass cylinders (from a type of petrol pump that has now disappeared from filling stations). These cylinders were joined by metal rings, the joints being sealed with a plastic compound. At the top was a hydrogen discharge-tube and, in spite of some inevitable leakage of gas from it into the main column, a good enough vacuum could be obtained by pumping from the bottom to prevent electrical breakdown within the stack. A well-directed beam of protons could then be made to strike a target within the column near its base. The apparatus is now in the Science Museum, London.

Alpha-particles from the $^{7}_{3}\mathrm{Li} + ^{1}_{1}\mathrm{H} \rightarrow ^{4}_{2}\mathrm{He} + ^{4}_{2}\mathrm{He}$ reaction were seen at once as soon as Cockcroft and Walton put a scintillation screen close to a target of lithium that was struck by the protons. Rutherford came down and was quite sure that the scintillations were indeed those of α-particles; as he said at the Royal Society meeting when Cockcroft and Walton described their work—"I know them; I was at their birth." What he said in conversation after the meeting was even more interesting: "I had to go and read the

The high voltage apparatus with which Sir John Cockcroft (1897–1967) and Ernest Walton (1903–   ) split atomic nuclei.

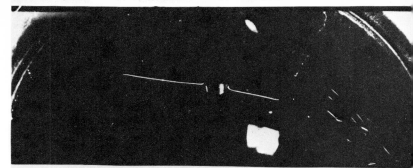

Tracks of two α-particles emitted in opposite directions during the bombardment of lithium by artificially accelerated deuterons

$$^6_3\text{Li} + {}^2_1\text{H} \longrightarrow {}^4_2\text{He} + {}^4_2\text{He} \quad (\text{Range} = 13.0 \text{ cm.}) \quad \dots (\text{i})$$

A similar photograph to the above shewing an opposite pair of α-particle tracks produced according to the reaction (i), together with a proton of long range emitted in the process

$$^6_3\text{Li} + {}^2_1\text{H} \longrightarrow {}^7_3\text{Li} + {}^1_1\text{H} \quad \dots\dots\dots\dots\dots (\text{ii})$$

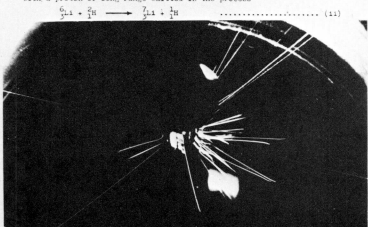

In this photograph the stopping power of the windows surrounding the target was 5.1 cm. instead of 10 cm., and the oppositely directed pairs of α-particles produced in reaction (i) pass out to the walls of the expansion chamber.

The inhomogeneous group of α-particles with ranges up to 7.8 cm. are produced in the process

$$^7_3\text{Li} + {}^2_1\text{H} \longrightarrow {}^4_2\text{He} + {}^4_2\text{He} + {}^1_0\text{n} \quad \dots\dots\dots\dots\dots (\text{iii})$$

Cloud-chamber photographs of particles emerging from nuclear reactions produced by (invisible!) neutrons.

85

Riot Act to these boys." Cockcroft and Walton could have seen the α-particles more than a year earlier, but they had first looked for γ-rays, and apparently it was Rutherford who pressed them to use the simple, old-fashioned scintillation counter. The old enthusiasm and authority were still there, and the jocular overstatement.

A few years later, Rutherford and his colleagues decided that the Cavendish Laboratory needed a cyclotron, a much more substantial and expensive piece of equipment. Cockcroft was put in charge of its design and construction, and it was arranged to build an almost identical one at Liverpool, where Chadwick had recently gone as Professor of Physics. These two machines marked the entry of engineering into British nuclear physics, and only Rutherford could have raised the funds for them, though they were tiny compared with what is built nowadays.

Both cyclotrons were successful, and the Liverpool one was in use until the 1960s. In the early 1950s, when Rutherford was dead and Cockcroft was directing the Atomic Energy Research Establishment at Harwell, the Cambridge cyclotron's magnet and power supply were transferred to Birmingham, where they formed the basis for a new type of cyclotron which is in active use, a pleasant reminder of the parts that Rutherford and Cockcroft played in the change-over from small-scale to large-scale nuclear physics.

Rutherford's last pieces of actual research were done with Oliphant. They decided to do with deuterons* what Cockcroft and Walton had done with protons: use them to bombard targets of the lighter elements and see what disintegrations took place.

They went for still larger currents, at lower voltages than Cockcroft and Walton had used. One of the reasons for this choice was that the discovery of the neutron had shown that a deuteron must be a neutron-proton combination. Its mass was very little

* Deuterons are the nuclei of "heavy hydrogen," which was discovered by Urey, an American physical chemist, in 1932.

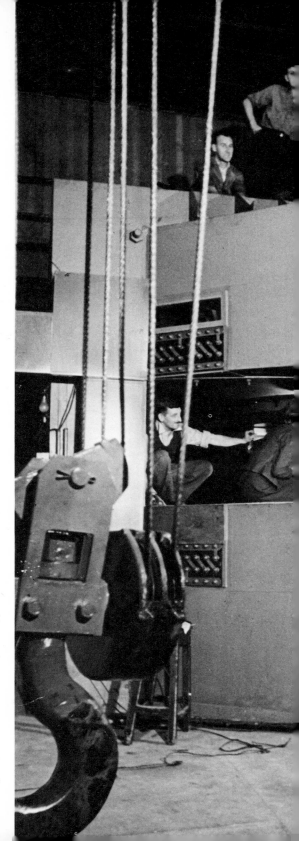

less than the sum of the masses of a neutron and a proton, and that meant, on Einstein's principle of the equivalence of mass and energy, that the two particles were only weakly bound to one another. The possibility of disrupting deuterons in low-energy collisions with other nuclei seemed high—and why not use deuterons as projectiles *and* target nuclei?

Oliphant and Rutherford were joined by a German physicist in this work, and later by an English student, but the technical achievement was essentially Oliphant's and the apparatus had a more professional look than Cockcroft and Walton's.

They found that two reactions took place when a target of "heavy ice" (D_2O) was bombarded:

$$\begin{array}{c} {}^2_1D + {}^2_1D \begin{cases} \longrightarrow {}^3_1H + {}^1_1H \\ \longrightarrow {}^3_2He + {}^1_0n \end{cases} \end{array}$$

and the outgoing particles (${}^1_0n$ is a neutron) had very high kinetic energies.

Left Magnet of the Nuffield Cyclotron at the University of Birmingham in 1945. Standing is Sir Mark Oliphant, directing operations.

Above Sir John Cockcroft (1897–1967) as Director of the Atomic Energy Research Establishment, Harwell, Berks, in July 1948.

Rutherford relaxing by the sea in Dorset, in about 1933, with his granddaughter, Elizabeth.

Rutherford with family and young friends on their summer holiday in Dorset in about 1933.

Though they could not know it (and Rutherford indeed once said: "Anyone who looks for a source of power in the transformation of atoms is talking moonshine") the results of these experiments were the basic starting-point for the "hydrogen bomb" and for what has not yet been achieved but may well come—the generation of useful power by controlled nuclear fusion.

Rutherford was more than an onlooker in this work, and he would not have allowed his name to be attached to the results if he had not made contributions to it; but it came last, not first, in the heading of the published paper.

He was, so to speak, signing off from a career of great brilliance, and leaving the future to his "boys." At that time, a large fraction of the world's active nuclear physicists had been with him in Manchester or Cambridge, and most of those who had not were students of those who had.

A generation after his death, he is remembered as the pioneer of nuclear physics and, in Einstein's words, "one of the greatest experimental scientists of all time, and in the same class as Faraday."

Chapter 1 of this account of his life and work began with two questioning lines from Wordsworth. For Rutherford, the reply comes best from Virgil: *Felix qui potuit rerum cognoscere causas* – "Happy is he who has managed to find out the causes of things."

Date Chart

1808	Dalton's atomic theory of chemical combination.
1833	Faraday's laws of electrolysis.
1868	Mendeléev's periodic table of elements.
1871	Rutherford born at Brightwater near Nelson, New Zealand, 30th August.
1890	Rutherford wins a scholarship to Nelson College.
1892	Rutherford wins a scholarship to Canterbury University College, Christchurch.
1893	Rutherford's M.A. degree.
1895	Rutherford's B.Sc. (honours) degree.
1895	Röntgen discovers X-rays.
1896	Becquerel discovers radioactivity.
1897	J. J. Thomson shows that electrons are independent particles.
1898	Rutherford is elected to the Macdonald Research Professorship of Physics at McGill University.
1898	Alpha- and beta-rays shown by Rutherford to be "distinct types of radiation."
1899	Rutherford notices thorium emanation.
1900	Planck's quantum theory of radiation put forward.
1902	Rutherford and Soddy discover the law of radioactive decay.
1903	Rutherford and Soddy see radioactivity as the transformation of atoms and suggest that alpha-particles are charged atoms of helium.
1903	Rutherford elected Fellow of the Royal Society.
1903	Crookes, and Elster and Geitel, independently notice scintillations in zinc sulphide. This leads to the construction of the scintillation counter.

1907	Rutherford appointed Langworthy Professor of Physics at the University of Manchester.
1908	Rutherford wins the Nobel Prize for Chemistry.
1911	Rutherford discovers the nuclear structure of atoms.
1911/13	Soddy, Russell, and Fajans recognize the existence of isotopes among radioactive elements.
1913	Bohr puts forward the quantum theory of atoms.
1913	Moseley verifies atomic numbers from X-ray spectra.
1914	Rutherford knighted.
1919	Rutherford achieves the first artificial disintegration of nuclei—the transmutation of the nitrogen nucleus by alpha-particle bombardment.
1919	Rutherford appointed Cavendish Professor of Physics at Cambridge and elected Fellow of Trinity College.
1924	De Broglie puts forward the wave theory of material particles.
1925	Rutherford awarded the Order of Merit. Elected President (1925–30) of the Royal Society.
1926	Greinacher counts alpha-particles using an ion chamber and amplifier.
1930	Rutherford created Baron Rutherford of Nelson.
1930	Lawrence and Livingston invent the cyclotron.
1932	Urey discovers deuterium.
1932	Chadwick discovers neutrons.
1932	Cockcroft and Walton achieve the transmutation of elements by protons.
1937	Rutherford dies at Cambridge, 19th October.

Further Reading

Rutherford, A. S. Eve (Cambridge University Press 1939)

Lord Rutherford, N. Feather (1940; reprinted Priory Press 1973)

Rutherford at Manchester, ed. J. Birks (Manchester University Press 1962)

Rutherford: The Cambridge Days, M. L. E. Oliphant (Elsevier 1972)

Notes and Records of the Royal Society of London, Vol. 27 No. 1

Glossary

ACTIVE DEPOSIT Radioactive layer left on surfaces exposed to emanation.

ANODE Positive electrode.

ATOMIC NUMBER The number that gives the place of an element in the periodic table and is the number of electrons in each atom of the element.

ATOMS The "building bricks" of all substances; an atom is the smallest particle of an element that can combine with other atoms to form molecules.

CATHODE Negative electrode.

CYCLOTRON A machine giving high energies to positive ions, guided in near-circular paths by a magnetic field and accelerated by a high-frequency voltage.

DEUTERIUM "Heavy hydrogen," having atoms twice as heavy as those of ordinary hydrogen.

DEUTERON Nucleus of deuterium atom.

DISCHARGE-TUBE A vessel containing low-pressure gas through which electric current is passed.

ELECTROCHEMICAL EQUIVALENT Equivalent weight in electrolysis.

ELECTRODES Plates or wires through which current passes to an electrically-conducting liquid or gas.

ELECTROLYSIS Separation of dissolved substances by an electric current.

ELECTROLYTE A substance which makes a solution electrically-conducting; or the solution itself.

ELECTROMETER An instrument for accurately measuring electric charges.

ELECTRONS Negatively-charged particles, forming the outer parts of all atoms.

ELECTROSCOPE An instrument for detecting, and roughly measuring, electric charges.

ELEMENT A substance that cannot be decomposed into chemically simpler substances.

EMANATION Radioactive gas; thoron (from thorium X), radon (from radium).

EQUIVALENT "The chemical equivalent of an element is the number of grams that will combine with, or will replace in chemical combination, one gram of hydrogen." This old fashioned definition will serve those readers who know very little chemistry; others will know its limitations, which do not matter for reading this book.

FARADAY Amount of charge carried by a gram-equivalent weight of ions in electrolysis, about 97,000 Coulombs.

ION Electrically-charged atom or group of atoms.

IONIZATION The production of ions, positive and negative, in a gas or other substance.

ISOTOPE One of two or more kinds of atom having the same chemical properties but different nuclear mass.

MOLECULE Two or more atoms when chemically combined with one another.

NEUTRON Neutral particle contained in all nuclei except (ordinary) hydrogen.

NUCLEUS The central part of every atom, positively charged and containing nearly all the mass of the atom.

NUCLIDE A particular species of nucleus.

PERIODIC TABLE Table of the chemical elements, arranged to show the regular recurrence of various properties.

PHOSPHORESCENCE The emission of light by a substance, *not* due to its being hot. (*Fluorescence* is the usual term if the light is emitted because other light has been shining on the substance).

PROTON Nucleus of (ordinary) hydrogen atom.

QUANTUM Literally, "a fixed amount;" in physics, an amount of energy fixed in proportion to the frequency of light (or X-rays or γ-rays) emitted or absorbed by an atom.

RADON Radium emanation.

SCATTERING A change of direction of particles, due to collisions.

SCINTILLATION A flash of light produced by a fast particle striking, for example, zinc sulphide.

SPECTRUM Originally, visible light, separated into the various colours that compose it; extended to mean the spread of *energies* among particles.

THORON Thorium emanation.

Index

Some illustrations of subjects and persons mentioned in the text are included in the index and marked with asterisks. References to Rutherford himself are not indexed.

Picture Credits

The author and publishers wish to thank all those who have given their kind permission for illustrations to appear on the following pages: Alexander Turnbull Library, NZ, 16; BBC Broadcasting House, 83; the Cavendish Laboratory, 35, 61, 72–73, 78, 82–83, 84–85; Central Electricity Generating Board, 9; Professor P. H. Fowler, 63, 64–65, 68–69, 88; Epoque Ltd., 25; Mansell Collection, 46–47, 56; Ministry of Defence, 10; National Portrait Gallery, *frontispiece*; Nelson Provincial Museum, NZ, 9, 14, 15, 52–53; His Excellency Sir Mark Oliphant, 22–23, 27, Paul Popper Ltd., 10, 36–37; Radio Times Hulton Picture Library, 38, 41, 44–45, 46–47, 70–71, 74, 85, 86–87, 87; Ronan Picture Library, 14, 26; Royal Institution, 21, 32–33, 39, 77; Royal Society, 21; Science Museum, 80–81; University of Canterbury, 17, 18–19.

We would especially like to thank His Excellency Sir Mark Oliphant and Professor P. H. Fowler for their help with illustrations, and John Elsegood for his work on the diagrams.